I0708327

BRAVE WOMEN AT WORK

Lessons in Confidence

BRAVE WOMEN AT WORK

Lessons in Confidence

JENNIFER PESTIKAS

Managing Editor
HOPE MUELLER

Contributors:

- Dr. Cindy Girman
- Dr. Belinda Hyppolite
- Dr. Amanda James
- Stephanie Joong
- Dr. Praba Koomson
- Jennifer Pestikas
- Marilyn Vetter
- Dr. Zenobia Tantra

Hunter Street
Press

DEDICATION

We dedicate this work to the brave young women, including our daughters, who are finding their full and confident selves.

"Woven with uncut honesty and striking personal stories, Brave Women at Work: *Lessons in Confidence* showcases the dangers of living a life for others while beautifully illustrating the power and opportunity in designing a life for yourself."

—**Tracy Porch**

"Confidence—this book tackles the journeys towards that tricky, often either elusive or falsely projected sense of assuredness about our place in the world. It portrays the myriad of ways we experience a lack of confidence and provides adventurous stories of how it has been and can be used to rebuild, generate, nourish, sustain, and abundantly applied in our lives to support the most important thing we can be—our Self, in this moment, in this place, at this point in time. The author's personal experiences of failure and successes with confidence create a woven map of what to reach for, what to look for, and what to lean into when you awaken at a crossroad of confidence in your own life. There is no cookie cutter approach here. There is, however, reach learning applicable to persons in all walks of life and in all kinds of circumstances."

—**Betsy Gornet**, President

"Confidence. When we look around the room, it's easy to assume everyone has it but us. We feel alone in our struggles, but we're not. Brave Women at Work: Lessons in Confidence, brings a community of support and inspiration to your fingertips. Through shared experiences, this book inspires you to take the next step in building your confidence in the workplace."

—**Amanda Phraner**, Sr. Director Product Communications

"There are many great takeaways in these pages. With explorations of how our personal foundations are established in our confidence and the importance of discovering our "why", *Lessons in Confidence* inspires thought. I don't remember curiosity as a catalyst for transformation & growth ever being so elegantly communicated. I walked away more determined to control my own path and with the tools to do so."

—**George Fiscus**, Owner, Managing Partner

CONTENTS

Prologue xiii

Introducing Marilyn Vetter.......................................1
   Why Not Me? 3

Introducing Stephanie Joong 19
   Reanimation 21

Introducing Dr. Praba Koomson 43
   The Knowing Within 45

Introducing Dr. Belinda Hyppolite 67
   You Are More 69

Introducing Dr. Cindy Girman 93
   Anxious Over-Achiever 95

Introducing Dr. Amanda James 119
   I've Got This! 121

Introducing Jennifer Pestikas............................143
   Imposter 145

Introducing Dr. Zenobia Tantra 165
   Confidence: Our Shining Jewel 167

Epilogue...189

Book Club Discussion Guide 193

Acknowledgements—Jennifer Pestikas................197

Acknowledgments—Hope Mueller 199

Other Publications by Hunter Street Press: 203

Excerpt from *Brave Women at Work: Stories of Resilience*...205

PROLOGUE

"Believe you can and you're half-way there."
— Theodore Roosevelt

As little girls, we are taught many things—be polite, be kind, be humble, be quiet, and do what you are told. These tenets follow us into high school, then college, then into the work force. We put in long hours at work, hoping someone will notice and eventually we might get recognized, or even promoted. We are polite and kind, even when we are uncomfortable or upset. We allow others to take credit for our ideas and often shrink in the face of opportunities or other challenges. We are missing a critical element of belief as Mr. Roosevelt says. We are missing confidence.

How do we manage the voice inside our heads that spews doubt, Imposter Syndrome, and fear? (Imposter Syndrome is a mistaken belief that one's success is fraudulent or merely lucky.) Fear that we are not enough. Fear that we cannot possibly be the right person for the job. Fear that we can't possibly balance it all. As a Hewitt Packard study states, "Men will apply for a job if they believe they meet sixty-one percent of the job qualifications; women will apply if they feel they meet one hundred percent."

While women are not alone in facing Imposter Syndrome or doubt, they often censor their actions at work as a result. According to an article in the Harvard Business Review on self- promotion at work, "Men rated their performance thirty-three percent higher than equally performing women." So, how do we grow our confidence and change the narrative?

We often learn confidence through personal and professional trials. Or perhaps we are fortunate enough to find a mentor or have family or friends that encourage us and reflect to us how talented, capable, and precious we are. Either way, we must make the decision to manage our inner critics to allow our true capabilities and gifts to shine. We must act in the face of fear. "We must feel the fear and do it anyway," as Susan Jeffers, psychologist and author, states. And by walking through these challenging situations, we engender self-confidence. And the more we face our fear and inner critic head on, the more confidence we gain.

The great news is that confidence can be gained by taking one small and bold move each day. Like picking up this book! As you read *Brave Women at Work: Lessons in Confidence*, you will hopefully find comfort and solace in that you are not alone on this journey. Managing our self-doubt, Imposter Syndrome, and feelings of fear are part of the human condition. All the authors that have graced us with their stories have faced similar struggles. As you will read, the brave women in this book did not let their inner critic or fears define them. They learned what we do with these feelings and that is what separates us from the rest.

INTRODUCING MARILYN VETTER

Marilyn is a leader of teams and developer of talent in the biopharmaceutical industry. She has jumped through hoops, climbed ladders, and dodged bullets in the professional gymnastics required to ascend in corporate America. Marilyn uses teachable moments, along with her intuition and ardor, to support other professional women.

Part of navigating the circuitous road to success is accepting that your confidence will not always be at its height. Giving herself grace to grow and to be vulnerable is a lesson Marilyn had to learn early and often, as she changed professions, roles, supervisors, and companies. While confidence is primarily an internal game, Marilyn knows that as leaders we can, and must, help employees, daughters, sons, and colleagues to hone their talents to become confident, energetic, and empowered leaders.

A spirit of service and volunteerism has guided Marilyn through a lifetime of philanthropy and nonprofit board roles, adding richness to her life while providing connections to community and causes. Her professional and personal worlds coincide in her current role as the President and CEO of Pheasants Forever and Quail Forever, the nation's leading organizations committed to conserving upland birds and wildlife through habitat improvement. Marilyn leads their dynamic 500-person organization and helps promote awareness of their critical work.

When she's not working, Marilyn enjoys traveling, writing, hiking, and hunting with her husband Clyde and their German shorthaired pointers.

Connect with Marilyn:
Facebook—Marilyn Vetter; Twitter—@vetter_marilyn
LinkedIn—linkedin. com/in/marilynvetter

WHY NOT ME?

"The executive team is working on succession planning." Chris looks up from his notebook and continues. "I'm struggling because Andrew isn't interested in my role. Let's brainstorm about people I should consider."

"Sure," I bobbed my head. Internally I buzzed and fretted. *Why did he ask Andrew first? Why didn't he ask if I was interested? Am I such a long shot that he wouldn't even consider me? What do I say?* I knew I could do the job and I wanted the opportunity to prove myself. I was not confident enough to ask for it right then.

I spent the next few weeks convincing myself Chris was not interested in elevating me as a candidate for the executive succession plan. My negative self-talk drowned out my confidence. Before our next one-on-one, I attended a luncheon for the Healthcare Businesswomen's Association Woman of the Year event. A colleague was being presented with an award in New York City, and the event was being broadcast to our headquarters.

During the event a speaker introduced the Honorable Mentor award winner. She shared how he played a crucial role in building her confidence. She told a story about him asking her to be his successor. She asked, "Why me?" and he replied, "Why not you?" He didn't understand how such a talented and competent woman couldn't see herself in the role. She went on to detail how he guided and prepared her to assume the next level of responsibilities. It was an example of someone seeing more in another person than they could see in themselves. The timing was serendipitous, reflecting my current situation. In that moment, I knew it was up to me to be confident enough to ask for the role.

I still have my notes from the luncheon where I wrote in all capital letters, "WHY NOT ME?" I left with the resolve and confidence to ask Chris that question. I psyched myself up throughout the week and during our next one-on-one, I took a deep breath and raised the topic of succession planning.

"Why not me?" I asked.

The room fell silent.

Chris looked down at his hands, then back at me, and said, "I didn't think you would want it." A grin spread across his face and he said, "Indeed, Marilyn, why not you?"

That single act and question changed our working relationship to one of mutual respect and growth. It was a reminder that no one could be a better advocate for me than—well, me! This series of events triggered months of reflection on why I wasn't considered for the job in the first place.

Deciding whom to promote or not commonly focuses on two elements: performance and potential. Both are subjective, but performance is less so because it is tied to goals and deliverables. Fascinating published gender research discusses how cisgendered males and females are perceived in terms of performance and potential. One study of a large North American retail chain found that although women in that organization were seven-point-four percent more likely to earn the top *performance* ratings, incongruently they were twelve percent more likely to be assigned the lowest *potential* rating, and sadly eighteen percent less likely to be rated as high *potential* candidates when compared to their male counterparts. Read those statistics again. Women are consistently rated as higher *performers* but somehow have less *potential* for promotion. The study showed thirty-three percent of women are "more likely than men to have the highest performance score and the lowest potential score." The study's authors referred to these candidates as "*workhorses.*" These study results reflect the reality of female leaders all around us and resonated with my experience and that of my network of female leaders and colleagues.

The study found that the gap was somewhat smaller, but still present, if the manager was female. Interestingly women rated all candidates, male and female, lower on potential than males. Perhaps females evaluate talent with the same difficult and high standards that we apply to ourselves.

This is particularly important because the study found that higher *potential* ratings were a stronger predictor for promotions than *performance*. In fact, the women in the study were thirteen percent less likely to be promoted than the men in the company even though they more frequently outperformed them.

Like many females, I thought working my tail off would give me visibility and move me to the top of the list for promotions. Silly me. It wasn't until later in my career that I realized I needed to advocate for myself and ask for promotions and raises, no one was going to hand them to me. *Why not me?* My male counterparts asked for raises and promotions without hesitation.

Parents, teachers, and employers need to teach all children and young professionals how to advocate for themselves early in their careers. Author and Yale Professor, Zoe Chance, attributes our inability to see women's potential in our society and culture because we associate leadership as a masculine trait. Chance's quote captures these findings perfectly, "Women feel forced to compete on their record, whilst men can compete on their vision."

The roots of my own self-doubt and lack of confidence are traced back to my formative years. I grew up on a small cattle ranch in central North Dakota. Because of our remote upbringing I was shy around strangers. At home I was a chatty, inquisitive child. In fact, my mother frequently said my first and favorite word was, "Why?" and apparently it still is.

At school I felt the stigma of being different and I had zero confidence. My handmade clothes and cheap haircuts didn't make me a popular girl. I did not know a single child in my kindergarten class. I did my best to hide and be invisible. I refused to play or engage with the kids in class. My teacher didn't tolerate my solitude for long. By the second week she thought a public spanking would force me out of my shell. I do not recommend or condone this traumatic technique to prompt a shy kid to engage in play. The experience hurt my confidence as a young child and forever instilled within me a fierce determination to earnestly avoid public humiliation, which has sometimes kept me rooted in fear. *Why not me?*

My fears didn't magically disappear, nor did my confidence magically grow. With practice I calmed my fears and began mustering my confidence. I excelled in choir and student government and was bold enough to run for and become class president in my junior year. My music instructors, guidance counselor, and some amazing teachers gently brought me out of my shyness, helped me face my vulnerabilities, and grow my self-esteem. Their belief in me planted the earliest seeds of confidence. I mastered my small-town fishbowl, but my burgeoning confidence was about to be challenged.

Going to a large public college resurfaced my old fears and my confidence wavered. I was there on a leadership scholarship yet internally I questioned my merit. I discovered it was easier to blend in and hide among the 11,000 students attempting to find their own ways and foster their own confidence than it was for me in my small kindergarten class. The Director of the School of Communications taught an Introduction to Communications class. The class was enthralling; I was immediately hooked. He saw something in me that I did not see in myself, a spark, a natural ability. This professor suggested I consider a career in broadcasting. Me? I am timid. I am shy. I could not imagine myself in front of a microphone and camera. *Why not me?*

I got outside my comfort zone and stood on shaky confidence. With effort and persistence, I found my niche. This was my jam. This career satiated my curiosity and allowed me to seek answers. My job was to find out who, what, where, and *why* and share the answers with the audience. I landed a reporter and anchor position at a Bismarck, ND television station. I covered politics and local news. I was in heaven. My skills improved and with them my confidence. You would be surprised to know how little most television personalities and reporters are paid. Then, and still now, they do not make a living wage. I needed to get a job that would pay the bills.

Although my confidence was growing, I was convinced I couldn't make it in a larger better paying market. Instead, I considered a career change. In reflection, I made this decision out of fear and a lack of confidence in myself. Instead of taking a chance in a larger market and risking failing, I gave up on this line of work, which I loved.

A friend was a pharmaceutical sales representative and said I would be great at it. *Why not me?* I was not as convinced and almost skipped the interview. If I had, I wouldn't have met my first district manager who was the next person who saw more in me than I saw in myself. He took a chance on a small-town communications major and reporter. His faith in me was the foundation on which I built my rewarding thirty-year biopharmaceutical career. In the process of abandoning one career, I nearly missed the opportunity for a second one out of fear and lack of confidence. *Why not me?*

Does confidence reside within us or is it bestowed upon us by the outside world? What is the source of our confidence? Is it entirely the belief in ourselves or can it be fostered by thoughtful and caring leaders, teachers, and parents who see our unique talents? I used to believe that if I doubted myself, it was because I was weak. I now realize it's not a sign of weakness; it's a sign of being human.

Confidence is built, sometimes through pain, sometimes through success, but always through learning. Confidence is not constant; it ebbs and flows with our level of proficiency. When we are in a new role, our curiosity is at its peak but our confidence in our abilities might not be commensurate. As we become more proficient our confidence grows. We all have times when we doubt our abilities. Those are the times we need others to lift us up and help us see our inner light and capability. *Why not you?* As leaders, we must be gracious with others, and ourselves, as our team members gain confidence and skills.

My early promotions came because of hard work and leaders who encouraged me to take the next step and advance. But I often waited for a permission slip from them first. I wonder where my career would have taken me if I had as much faith in myself as my early bosses did.

My early lack of confidence is common in young women. A study by Jack Zenger and Joseph Folkman of the leadership development consultant team Zenger Folkman and published in the Harvard Business Review details the gender confidence gap and how it shifts throughout life. In their study, women were rated higher by their managers in all categories but two. When asked to rate themselves, the women consistently rated themselves lower. When they compared confidence ratings for men and women, the biggest differences were in workers under twenty-five. By the time men and women were in their forties, their self-ratings were nearly equal. When both genders reached sixty, women's confidence ratings surpassed the men's ratings, which declined. Men's self-reported confidence ratings increased a mere eight-point-five percent from twenty-five to sixty years, while women's ratings jumped twenty-nine percent. Men start at a much higher confidence level and maintain a steady attitude about confidence throughout life.

Through guidance, encouragement, and recognition we can help fortify the confidence of young women earlier in their careers. Train them to ask for promotions, negotiate salaries, seek advancement without waiting for permission. An ability to advocate for themselves will dramatically change their career trajectories and earning potential and improve their overall quality of life. Advocating for oneself in all areas, not just work, is a powerful skill we want to see young women develop earlier.

When I chose not to pursue opportunities, what might have looked like a lack of confidence, was a fear of failure. I turned down promotions or job offers because I feared the unknown. *Why not me?* I chose the safe route more times than I care to admit in these pages about being a Brave Woman at Work.

I am not alone in choosing the safe path. Author and expert on women's leadership, Tara Sophia Mohr, sought to validate the findings of an often cited but rarely documented statistic from a Hewlett Packard internal report that indicated men apply for a job when they meet sixty percent of the qualifications, but women apply only if they meet all the qualifications. Mohr's research showed that the differences between men and women were much more nuanced. In fact, if men and women thought they weren't qualified for a position, most of both genders said they didn't apply because it was a waste of their time. Twenty-two percent of women said they didn't apply for a role for which they didn't meet the qualifications "because I didn't want to put myself out there if I was likely to fail." Only thirteen percent of men replied in the same way. Another fifteen percent of women said they didn't apply because they were following the rules of who should apply, when only just over eight percent of men gave that same response.

In March 2019, LinkedIn released their *Gender Insights* report to investigate how women and men use LinkedIn differently when looking for jobs. Their research validated the various studies on how both genders apply for work. When genders reviewed similar jobs, women were less likely to apply for a job as compared to men. According to the LinkedIn study one of the benefits of women's selectivity is that they are sixteen percent more likely to be hired when they apply for a position. When you question whether you are the right person for the role, remind yourself it's not your decision to make. Get past your fear and put yourself out there. The hiring manager decides who is the right fit for the job, not you.

Could these findings be more reflective of women

being less risk averse and because of societal pressure for girls to follow rules? Do we unwittingly hold ourselves back in the hopes of avoiding failure? Men are not immune to self-doubt or insecurity. The difference is they don't let it hold them back. This is an important lesson we can learn from our male counterparts. When you are riddled with self-doubt and insecurity, ask yourself, "*What is the worst that can happen?*" Rarely are the ramifications of failure so consequential that it's not worth trying. At the very least, you'll learn from the experience and know what not to do next time. Perhaps the best way to face doubt is to ask yourself, "*What is the BEST that could happen?*" Imagine all you can learn from being fearless and all that you can add to the world. *Why not you?* Leaders, teachers, and parents help young women build resilience and independence. These skills are the foundation of confidence.

When I was approached to write a chapter for this book on confidence, my stomach flipped, and I asked myself *Why me?* Leadership, developing teams, and transformation all seemed like logical topics for me to write about, but this characteristic of confidence has always vexed me. To help me evaluate the opportunity of being in this book, I asked a few peers what they most appreciated about working with me. They used words like courageous, doggedly supportive of my team, empathetic, and inspiring. *Why not me?* All of them thought it entirely rational that I should write about confidence. Women can have incredibly successful careers and still question their worth. I'm living proof of that.

As I was writing this chapter, I contemplated applying for a CEO role for a large nonprofit. I took a couple of months to decide if I should apply. Everyone in my network encouraged me to go for it. Like the women in the statistics above, I initially held back because I didn't meet *all* the qualifications. *Why not me?*

A critical part of the application process was providing written responses on my leadership style, accomplishments, examples of transformations I had led, how I had overcome adversity, my approach to developing teams, strategic planning, and fiduciary responsibilities. I wrote a six-page document in two hours. When I proofread it, I was astounded at how easily I came up with profound examples for each topic. I recommend this exercise to everyone. Once it's on paper, you appreciate all that you've achieved. It is a fabulous confidence builder—look at what I can do!

With intentional actions we elevate our confidence levels. The first step is to give ourselves grace when our self-esteem has taken a hit. It's okay to be disappointed by a lost promotion, project, or pay hike. But we can't stay back there in self-pity. Use that energy to pursue a new role or create an action plan of how to be ready for the next promotion. Having a plan will lift your spirits, ward off the feeling of being helpless, and propel you forward. *Why not you?*

Remind yourself that you are not alone. It's in these times we need to access our supporters. In LinkedIn's *Gender Insights* report, they discovered that women are twenty-six percent less likely than men to ask for a referral, even when they have a connection at the company. That self-limiting behavior serves no one, including your future employer, who could benefit from your talent. *Why not you?*

If you have opportunities for growth, identify ways to bolster your professional skill set. Ask your supervisor, coworkers, and friends if they have ideas on how you could grow professionally. See if your employer will fund a 360-survey to enrich your self-awareness. Don't take the survey's feedback personally. This exercise is meant to help you find ways to improve, not beat yourself up. *Why not you?*

If you use a lot of verbal pauses like "um, ah, er" or have a fear of public speaking, ask your employer for a coach. If that's not possible, find a Toastmasters Club to hone your skills and ask your friends to remind you when they notice you using these filler words. Use your phone to record yourself when you are presenting or are on conference calls to monitor your progress. *Why not you?*

Give yourself a pep talk before getting on an important call with leaders to make sure your attitude is upbeat and optimistic. If you're the person who never asks a question in a meeting, make a list of potential questions ahead of time so that you don't have to think on your feet. You do not have to pretend you are a totally different person. Enhancing your communication skills is a basic step to improving your comfort level, your self-esteem, and your confidence and it's a basic tenet of success. The same goes for your writing skills or other technical skills like creating power points. If they aren't your strengths, take a class to ensure you are adept and comfortable in the areas that otherwise feel intimidating to you. *Why not you?*

Confidence is what you project to the world about how you feel about yourself and your abilities. Do everything you can to portray strength, empathy, innovation, and intellect in a way that is authentic to you.

Finally, focus on the skills you possess when you are applying for a new position. *Why not you?* Remind yourself they aren't looking for a unicorn that possesses 100% of the skills laid out in the job description. Use your cover letter to bridge any perceived skill gaps in your work history if your resume doesn't overtly state it. Tap into your contacts who can endorse you on LinkedIn and make connections to the hiring manager or leaders within the company.

It is ironic that during the writing of this chapter I was applying for a CEO position. The irony is that I experienced many of the emotions that erode confidence like self-doubt, fear of failure, and insecurity about my abilities throughout the process and even before applying. My history of fear kicked in, but this time I pushed fear aside and guess what? I got the job! And you can too. I am headed into another great unknown with excitement and confidence. *Why not me?*

Fear-demons and self-doubt are created to protect us when perhaps they are needed. It's important to know when they no longer serve you. When you're questioning yourself whether you are good enough; calm, and center yourself, take a deep breath, listen to your internal dialogue, and ask yourself *Why not me?* The universe will answer you so be prepared when it says, "Why not indeed!"

INTRODUCING STEPHANIE JOONG

Stephanie Joong is a pharmaceutical leader and medical device innovator, a distance runner, and an avid science, technology, engineering and math (STEM) promoter. A trained and degreed engineer, she has taken roles of increasing responsibility, leading organizations, and broadening her purview across the business landscape. Stephanie holds a B. S. in Chemical Engineering from Bucknell University, an M. Eng. in Biochemical Engineering from Lehigh University and has completed her MBA at the Kellogg School of Management, Northwestern University. Stephanie has a strong desire to collaborate across cultures and aspires to have a global impact in her industry.

Stephanie volunteers for the Society of Women Engineers (SWE), a mentor network where she provides situational coaching for college students, those early in their careers, and women seeking career changes. She is committed to promoting women in STEM and hopes to see women continue advancing into senior roles especially in corporate settings. She believes in paying forward the life-changing mentorship she has received.

Stephanie enjoys making new running friends, taking local hikes, backpacking in the wilderness, and international travel with her husband, Aaron. She calls Oakland, California home.

REANIMATION

We stood in the grey conference room, shifting our weight or leaning against the wall with folded arms. Standing room only for our team. The senior executives invited the Extended Leadership Team to hear an announcement from our Plant Manager and her boss. I had never seen him in person and thought *This is not normal.* In Northern California we were far away from the home office and the plant didn't attract much outside attention. Curiously the meeting was scheduled minutes before our site's Town Hall where a murmuring crowd was already gathering and settling into their seats a few doors away.

Our manufacturing plant was closing.

I heard but did not listen to the words. I scanned the faces of my colleagues. I wasn't sure which facial expression I should be wearing or what was appropriate in this setting. *I was a leader, (wasn't I?) and should just nod in understanding. Look solemn.*

A supervisor behind me started to cry. She shared her anguish aloud. She looked at and acknowledged each of us, including the bearers of the news. *That's a bit dramatic. I can't imagine crying at work, especially in front of colleagues.* Our jobs would be eliminated over the next four years throughout the process of closing the site. I was shocked into silence in a fog of disbelief. I was recently promoted to Facilities Manager. This position was my first assignment with direct reports and leading people, and I was only just getting the hang of it.

We weren't done yet. Now the Plant Manager had to share the news with the rest of our people, and I, still numb to what was happening, would have to help lead my people through the change.

We were herded into the cafeteria where the three hundred site employees waited. I was early in my career and didn't see this coming, but most others weren't surprised. I had been at the site only three years whereas most of the others were far more tenured. Their roots, families, and community were here. The layoffs would come in waves. The decision was final and publicly communicated yet we were nowhere near the end. We still had to produce products, deliver on our commitments, and meet our customers' needs while we embarked on the decommissioning. I had a new role to play.

My life up to this point had been defined by my educational and career successes. This is who I was, and my confidence was grounded in this identity. I was a successful young professional with a long runway ahead of me. My career aligned with my college degree, in a well-paying, recession-proof industry. Sure, there were other interests and hobbies, but none of them defined me nor how I presented myself. I outwardly exuded confidence. Enjoying hobbies took a backseat to my job and, truth be told, so did my family.

I had moved cross-country for this opportunity and said goodbye to friends and family. I sold my condo. And my boyfriend, Aaron, quit his job to move with me. We explored San Francisco, the Bay Area, and the great outdoors of California—an East Coaster's dream. We joined recreational sports leagues and embarked on new friendships. Aaron and I got engaged, married, and bought our first home together. All those chapters were built on the foundation of this job, my main concern. I was checking the boxes of what a confident and successful life looked like and I was on pace to achieve some imaginary perfect life. In the weeks and months after the announcement, I questioned my choices, and my confidence faltered. *What was the point of all this? My resume is forever tarnished.* The life we built was minimized, even trivial.

I believed no one would hire me because I was a failure. I had never been fired from a job. Intellectually I knew the difference between a lay-off and a dismissal with cause, but I couldn't help believing it was somehow my fault, my shortcoming. In my own mind, I minimized the work I had already contributed as an Engineer since being there and I reduced my achievements to nothing.

Raised in an Asian American household, my expectations to achieve ran high from an early age. The younger of two daughters to Taiwanese immigrants, I had a lot to live up to. I was driven, self-motivated, and while my parents were proud of my accomplishments, they rarely vocalized this to me without solicitation. As an adult I adopted perfectionist traits, which had nothing to do with reaching perfection but all to do with never being satisfied, always needing to attain the next level. Stepping into corporate America right after college further fueled this competitive mindset. I was taught to push down my insecurities and plow through with determination.

Thinking about losing this job took up all the space within me. I didn't allow myself to enjoy anything, my confidence was zero. I was unworthy and carried the weight of my perceived failure everywhere. An extended family trip to the breath-taking scenery of snowy Whistler (a popular British Colombia destination), did not shake my lingering sadness. Backpacking trips to Yosemite, which usually left me in awe, had little impact on my mood. I was drifting away and felt isolated and alone, even in the company of family and friends.

Around my family I only knew how to communicate just the facts of what was happening with work. A lifetime of suppressing my feelings and pretending to have thick skin led to a gap in my communication skills to tell them my life was crumbling and there was no way to fix it.

To make matters worse I stopped doing the activities I enjoyed altogether, like distance running. I began this sport after I finished my first master's degree, in Biochemical Engineering, which I completed while working full time. When the program was done, I filled the educational void with yet another challenge. I routinely ran local half-marathons to discover the communities surrounding me. I was disciplined in training, set predictable routines, prioritized working out and grew confident in my ability. I ran with other serious runners for accountability and comradery. I completed the San Francisco marathon, my first, a few minutes under four hours one year before the site closure announcement. Without exercise, though, I stopped feeling like myself and my confidence wilted.

My mental state revealed itself in physical changes.

I gained fifteen pounds from closeted emotional eating. There was a gas station down the street from my office that had a well-stocked convenience store for truckers coming off Route 80. There I bought piles of junk food, family sized Nacho Cheese Doritos, charged to my personal credit card so Aaron couldn't see, and routinely consumed entire bags while driving to and from work. My skin was dull, my face bloated. Acne bloomed on my cheeks from the garbage food and my decline in personal hygiene. I wanted to make myself smaller and hide. *If people saw me, what would they think?* They might be concerned about my health and the fact that I stopped all efforts to maintain appearances. They might ask questions that shamed me to answer.

I was a shell of myself. Faded and listless, my reaction time was slow. It was difficult to follow basic instructions or carry simple conversations even outside of work. I felt unsafe driving because I had no reflexes. Once I hit a deer that appeared out of nowhere in broad daylight on a back-country road, substantially damaging my car, and forcing me to replay the event in my mind nonstop. *If I wasn't so distracted, would I have seen it coming?* My fifty-five-mile commute was consumed by my overanalyzing brain and flogging myself for the circumstances I got myself into.

At work, I could barely function. Shortly after the

announcement I advanced onto the Senior Leadership Team. I was the youngest manager so maybe they thought my behavior was growing pains tied to inexperience, a phase that everyone goes through. Or maybe they thought I was overwhelmed by the workload. It was more severe than that. I managed an entire department; it was a critical role with expanded responsibilities due to the site closure. Yet there were days I couldn't even show up to work and instead stayed in bed. *And I had been the one to judge another for shedding tears in that initial, shattering closure announcement event.*

A close colleague, Katrina, often covered for me. I didn't even ask her to. She was compassionate and saw my struggle for what it was. Katrina asked how my days were, but we never spoke directly about my depression. My mentor, Blake, refers to this period as my disconnected phase. On the surface I was like any stressed-out manager struggling to keep all the balls in the air. Internally I lost my sense of identity and couldn't summon even one forward step to bring me out of my hopelessness. I am surprised I wasn't fired.

Further, I lost my creativity, even ordering food was difficult. Nothing satisfied me, it was all bland. Aaron grew more and more concerned, and, standing on the sidelines, he didn't know how to help. I believed I was responsible for the site shutting down. He knew I started to see a therapist for the first time, and we both hoped that would turn things around.

I oscillated between abject nothingness and pure mania.

Frantically, I applied to any job that I was remotely qualified for. I threw my resume across the internet at positions with the word "engineer" or "manager" in them. I undersold myself in desperate attempts to secure anything, even easier roles with fewer skills. I cast a wide net, excessively clicking the Easy-Apply button on LinkedIn regardless of the position.

I thrust myself into researching new hobbies that might awaken some interest, some spark, anything. This frenzied period included me considering buying and running a glamping campsite with yurts, an escapist move to New Zealand to raise sheep for sweater knitting, creating jobs in sustainable aquaculture, or starting an urban farm, fundraising to benefit low-income housing, and learning Chinese and Japanese, simultaneously, for a future corporate job abroad. These frantic searches came to nothing. Even the sheep farms and knitting failed to lift my creative spirits.

I sourced and bought the Chinese and Japanese textbooks and hired a tutor before I gave up because my brain wasn't working, and I couldn't absorb information. These were desperate attempts at finding where I belonged, finding my confidence. I watched days go by without being an actual part of them. I tried running again. I secured a dedicated running partner, Harry, from the San Francisco marathon training program, paid the entry fee for the Avenue of the Giants marathon, then dropped out and left him to prepare alone. I was a failure *and* a bad friend.

Despite my inner turmoil, the disconnected thoughts, and my downward spiral, I hid most of it from the professional world. I received a job offer for an externally facing operations role with interesting challenges at the same company. It did not include managing people, though, and the salary increase wasn't meaningful. But this opportunity, this consideration, was a first chance for positive self-reflection. Even though I was flailing about for opportunities, when one came, the specifics of the job did not feel right.

Then some sane part of my brain woke up. I realized that in fact I wanted a job with direct people management. I wanted to lead and develop people, to keep growing in this area, otherwise I wouldn't be fulfilled. This was my first step out of the fog. I realized bouncing from interview to interview was premature; I still had so much more to learn. Instead of continuing my manic job search, I decided to focus my efforts on furthering my education. Investing in myself would help me grow, gain insight into what made me tick, and create a new career plan.

I was accepted into the Kellogg School of Management at Northwestern University, my top choice, and conjured up the courage to ask my senior leaders for the financial support and the time needed to maximize an Executive MBA program. The ongoing career chats I had with my leadership paid off. None of them were surprised and they approved and funded my MBA. This was a big win, a second step on my path back to health and confidence.

In the aftermath of the site closure announcement, I was responsible for keeping engagement levels high and delivering on our customer promised volumes throughout this winding down period. Now that I'd taken a few steps forward, the daily challenges and conversations at work were easier, which proved to be another step in the right direction. My department consisted of experienced and tenured professionals and our operating norms were well established. Now, three years into the role, I put my education at the top of my priorities because my position and my employees were stable, and we managed to operate with few surprises.

I delegated more responsibilities to the team to focus on my education and my resulting reanimation. The team understood. I was transparent with my travel and coursework commitments. I shared with my team what I enjoyed learning, which topics were most difficult, and where I could see myself going at the end of this program. This approach aligned with our company's dedication to each impacted employee finding her next step. I shared a lot about myself. I learned that professionalism and authenticity could coexist.

Looking back, my first reaction to the site closure announcement prevented me from seeing the stability brought with the decision. We, the site leaders, knew what was going to happen; there was no ambiguity. This straightforward direction allowed steadfast prioritization, organization, and eliminated unnecessary activities that are common when running a business. There were fewer yet crisper goals and less competing priorities. In retrospect, this clarity and stability were a gift which paved the way for me to focus on educational commitments.

I attributed my first and only easy win during school, a basic statistics course, to my Engineering background. However, immediately after that, the difficulty of learning shot up. Courses like Accounting, Marketing, Finance, and Strategy were foreign to me even though I thought I was practicing aspects of these in my job already. My instinctive answers were off by big margins, and I couldn't rely on intuition to get by. Within a month I was defeated. *What made me think I was smart enough to do this? Did I take a spot in this educational cohort from a more deserving student out there?*

In March 2020, COVID-19 shut down the country. I flew home early from my weekend of classes and faced an emergency slate of work responsibilities upon arrival. I was a critical contributor to the Crisis Management Team formed to address the new and changing realities of COVID-19. Keeping our employees safe was our singular purpose. We pored through the latest CDC information, the news, and our company's own reports to rapidly develop policies and procedures.

At the same time anti-Asian sentiment exploded into my world with local hate crimes and violent incidents close to my home, which made me question my safety. Asian hate crimes forced me to keep a low profile and shrink into the background to preserve my wellbeing. Asian-looking people were harassed, shoved to the ground, and even killed in their own communities in misguided retaliation for the so-called "China Flu." The times were oppressive and scary, and I found it even more difficult for me to act decisively during this time. However, the momentum and undeniable reality of the pandemic, the associated violence and threat of personal safety, forced me to see what was important. Fueled by the injustice, with a renewed sense of purpose, I actively focused on the wellbeing of others, which was my third major step out of my depression which helped me regain my self-confidence.

Throughout the two-year MBA program, I worked on all my assignments in a small group with six others, a curated team established in calculated, yet unknown, ways by the university. The faculty called us Team H and we keep in touch by that name in our text messaging group today. Through coursework and facilitated reflections I learned about my new teammates. We each grappled with our own set of external and internal pressures, priorities to manage, and changing career ambitions all interwoven with no shortage of moments where we felt inadequate—we were vulnerable together. We explored new jobs, promotions, international moves, and growing families. We also experienced illness, loss, frustration, and soul searching together.

As a group of seven we had the gift of taking turns leading assignments and giving short breaks to anyone who was going through a particularly difficult stretch at the office, with their families, or simply traveling on a much-needed vacation. We valued each other's well-being far greater than academic grades. For each topic or assignment, we identified the team's subject matter expert and trusted them to lead the way. We took turns leading and following, which was more efficient and productive than trying to bulldoze our way through all the work on our own.

Handling the COVID crisis, I was stretched and constantly connected to work. But I also kept my focus, leaning on my coaches, my classmates, and my therapist, and drawing from a surprising well of resilience. Our crisis team bonded together to face the common enemy threatening our community workplace. My COVID-19 story was shaped by the role I held at the time of the lockdown, my educational commitments, and my struggle to pull myself out of the deepest alternate reality I'd ever experienced by being of service to my friends, classmates, and colleagues. The job multiplied overnight, creating the impetus that pulled me out of my doomed state. I realize now that I pushed myself hard in the right areas and contributed meaningfully. With my words, decisions, and actions I had an impact on hundreds of peoples' lives.

I hold a special place for these salient moments during the pandemic at the plant. I sat, defeated, in an empty second-story conference room which looked out to a magnificent palm tree, sifting through a huge binder of our (unhelpful) response plan for disease outbreaks. I devoted way too much time to making an extensive, color-coded spreadsheet separating our workforce into two populations to prevent disease spread, ensuring entire departments wouldn't be sick at the same time by staggering their onsite work hours.

While it didn't serve my individual best interests, I assigned Katrina to the opposite team from me so we could divide the support across our combined employees. We went months only seeing each other on laptop screens. For personal contact, I played afternoon games of ping pong with my mentor Blake, who was promoted to Plant Manager by then. We sanitized the paddles between use and justified the length of the table between us as a safe distance. We didn't remove the ping-pong table because that was where we did our best reflecting and feedback sessions. These snippets remind me that as a leader, as a human, I helped in seemingly small ways during a time of immense despair. More importantly now, even when I wasn't certain of my abilities, I made the choice to keep showing up and to lead with confidence.

Back at school, beyond my small team, was an extensive ecosystem of support: I felt heard and respected during lectures. I was given the stage when I voiced my ideas or drew upon examples from my experience during class regardless of my age, gender, race, industry, or title. By the time I graduated I was unstoppable—I gained a clearer picture of who I was, what I was capable of, and what I had to offer. In today's working world few goals, if any, are achieved solo. *Why couldn't I take the team dynamics l learned in school and apply them to my job?* I directed my efforts into creating complementary teams versus attempting to prove my worth alone. In fact, throughout my journey from the start of this story, I was never alone, I just didn't recognize the support around me.

I took charge of new work responsibilities, and I noticed the difference. When Katrina landed an exciting new job abroad, I welcomed yet another change of responsibilities by inheriting her Engineering and Maintenance team. I was active in planning that change and was eager to learn how to best support this new team. I struck a new balance managing the energy devoted to my now online schoolwork and elevating my performance at work. I was much better equipped to evaluate new roles and opportunities for myself, which I now was certain would be within this company and not external.

Suddenly a five-minute meeting from a Supply Chain Vice President slipped onto my calendar with short notice. He was the hiring manager for a role for which I had applied and interviewed; Blake had forwarded the posting with the note "This might interest you." No virtual meeting link, he'd call me directly on my cell. I interviewed three panelists virtually. *A five-minute call? That's long enough to tell a candidate they didn't get the job, right?*

I got the job.

I was promoted into an operations role in the San Francisco Bay Area. Although this was an internal move, it was a significant change. The role was in medical devices and not pharmaceuticals. It was a new facility, with new people and broader responsibilities. At one time this call and the new role would have terrified me. Now, I felt redeemed, reanimated, confident. I knew this was the right move for me. I could do something different and even if I made mistakes along the way I could advance myself and my career.

What really mattered was that the new job allowed me to finish the remaining five months of my MBA (and put my new skills into practice). I would be launching a new production line from scratch, the cleanest slate I have ever been given. It granted me broader exposure and fresh networking opportunities as well.

Since it was in the Bay Area, I didn't need to relocate, sell my house, worry about who was taking the dogs, or disrupt the life Aaron and I had created. I kept my friends and support systems close by. As a bonus, my father, mother, and sister all moved closer to California during the pandemic. It had been decades since we all lived in the same time zone. My support network grew and with it my confidence. I gave myself permission to keep aspects of my life easy, an alien concept for me up until then.

I am grateful for my role in the site's closure. It was terrifying in the beginning and completely out of my control. It was a triggering event which disassembled the identity I had painstakingly created. I took the terrible news badly and entered an even worse, drawn-out nightmare. At one point my therapist told me that I was not the cause of the global pandemic. That is how much I piled onto my back and how dismal a reality my mind had contrived. It is an understatement to say I was too hard on myself.

I built confidence through this period of depression. It was hard-won and started with identifying and acknowledging something that I did not want. I didn't want to accept a position that didn't include leading people. I appreciated the transparency and ease afforded to me and my organization through the announcement of the plant closure. With a strong team and established processes, I focused on developing myself further through education and learned the tools to increase my self-awareness. My MBA experience brought about the discovery of my increased value through a new network. I was even given help with an expertly curated cohort. Most weekends it was in this place where I sought refuge—I depended on it. I consistently tried to provide stability and continuity to my employees, but I needed my own rock to lean on. Then the pandemic hit and my relentless focus on the greater good of our employees drove me across the finish line, leaving the dark days behind.

I graduated business school confident that wherever I landed I'd be more than fine, I'd navigate through it and extract the best out of the circumstances. My view of the word "opportunity" evolved. Until then, opportunity was used to soften the blow of incoming constructive feedback. Now, opportunity is seeing ways to make things better that perhaps most others couldn't see and then having the skills, coupled with courage, to make it happen.

I used each incremental win to boost me to my next challenge and I knew when I was ready. I took on more and more risks as my confidence grew and my fear of failure waned. Ascending from the darkness, I gained a clearer head and more reserves of confidence. I recognized that my value, my worth, my very identity were not defined by my educational and career success. I was a whole person, with strengths and weaknesses, interests, and desires. Now I have agency. Now I carry less of a burden and allow myself to enjoy life. By experiencing crippling depression, I can empathize with the desperation and sadness in others. I offer kindness and share what worked for me without shame.

Self-confidence is not only being comfortable in my skin, but also not wanting to trade mine for anyone else's. I'm dialed in to who I am and what's going to make me complete. It's astounding how one incident played such a central role in my life, unfolding more and more decision branches with many more choices. I am unrecognizable from who I was three years ago. What I possess now is so valuable: I'm reanimated and filled with a new thirst for living. These days I have a brilliant color that radiates off me—it is genuine, effortless, and something I'm proud I created.

After several years of inconsistent physical exercise, I wanted a redo at that failed marathon in the Redwoods, too. I texted Harry, "I think I'm going to sign up for next year's Avenue of the Giants Marathon. It's the day after my birthday". Without any questions or reference to my previous inability to follow through he responded, "Time to revive our original training plan," and we picked up where we left off. We signed up for the race in 2022, this time with two more of our friends. As I trained, I realized that each run cleared the noise from my head, and both my body and mind grew stronger. My sister drove five hours with her friends to cheer us on with big hand-drawn signs and over-the-top noise makers. We made a weekend of it: rented a big house, cooked group meals, and celebrated my thirty-fifth birthday.

I am not alone. I am loved. I am a powerhouse, a young professional. I have many choices ahead of me. I cannot wait to see what I do next.

INTRODUCING DR. PRABA KOOMSON

Dr. Praba Koomson is a talented leader with experience across the healthcare continuum. She has proven expertise in implementing strategic, operational, and innovative approaches to care delivery in diverse settings. Dr. Koomson has trained and worked in Ghana, the United Kingdom, and the United States. Praba specializes in interprofessional collaborative practice, with a focus on population health, healthcare innovation development, practice research, and leadership development.

Praba is an educator driven to inspire the pursuit of academic and personal excellence by creating challenging and engaging learning environments to promote life-long practitioners and scholars. She is an expert in developing and implementing educational technology tools and applications to support diverse educational settings at the graduate and doctoral levels. Praba has a special interest in models of care that address the health and well-being of the chronically and seriously ill population, with special emphasis on the role of shared decision-making approaches in enhancing patient-centric care. Praba speaks nationally and internationally on diverse healthcare topics that cover a range of health and social care issues. Praba is passionate about how care delivery aligns with the choices, values, and preferences of individuals and communities.

In honor of her mother, Professor Hannah Victoria Koomson, Praba established The HanVick Corporation, a non-profit organization dedicated to supporting and educating patients and caregivers in navigating health and social care ecosystems. HanVick partners with other organizations and faith communities in Ghana to educate and support the delivery of care for homebound elders, families with special needs and mental health clients.

Praba loves to travel with her family, to learn about other cultures, especially how individuals and communities in diverse settings maintain their health and wellness in alignment with their cultural identity.

THE KNOWING WITHIN

My name is Praba Koomson. I am the daughter of Hannah Victoria Koomson and the ancestral grandchild child of the Reverend Pra Koomson. This is my core uniqueness: who I am, where I am from, the foundational mapping of my lineage, and the community of people with whom I belong. My identity, my roots, my lineage, my clan, and the intersectionality of these four elements provide the framework of my being. This deep and immeasurable knowing within me of who I am is fundamental to my very existence, and the first building block of my self-confidence.

Born in Ghana, per tradition I did not possess an identity until seven days after birth. Till the seventh day, I was a being, concrete, solid, real, but with no ties to anything, other than an irrefutable biological tie to Hannah Victoria Koomson, my mother. On day seven I became a human being with a unique identity, rooted in my lineage, my clan, and the community of people with whom I belonged.

I became Praba Koomson. My own name was my first achievement in life. As is Ghanian tradition, I was named after an ancestor. We are not named after just any ancestor, but an ancestor worthy of emulation, an individual of high regard, worthy of admiration, and a bastion of the community. The precise goal of this tradition is to provide a role model for each individual child, a person who provides ongoing guidance and support, who holds you accountable in all aspects of your life, who connects you with your clan and community, who holds you up in times of trouble, and provides you with a pathway to success.

Such an ancestor was my grandfather; the Reverend Pra Koomson, a man of talent, compassion, lauded skill as a renowned traditional healer, and a succor to his community. And so, I became Pra-[ba] which means child of Pra, and accordingly, I too have become a woman of talent and compassion and am a healer. I have a doctorate degree in the healing profession of nursing. I specialize in inter-sector, inter-agency, and inter-disciplinary practice. As a nurse educator, I provide knowledge and skill to the individuals, communities, and colleagues that I serve. This respectfully reflects my professional lineage, professional clan, and my community.

I share this level of specificity and formality because it is the basis of my journey in confidence. The foundation of confidence is built upon knowing who I am, deeply and irrefutably. It is in knowing and understanding all aspects of myself that I can credibly connect to and understand my successes, failures, aspirations, and achievements. This allows me to candidly share myself and my story in a meaningful way. I propose this knowledge of self as the primary factor for developing self-confidence and self-worth, which we know to be a predictor of success.

Hannah Victoria Koomson was my esteemed mother. She was a paragon of good works and notable achievements. As a child of illiterate parents, my mother obtained a full-ride scholarship to Bath College of Education in England and completed her baccalaureate work as a family life educator. After completing her baccalaureate, she secured a full-ride scholarship to Cornell University in Ithaca NY for further post-graduate work. She was initially a lecturer and then was named Dean of the Family Life Education department at our local university. She was well-loved by her students and her community. She was the first president of the Methodist Church of Ghana, Women's Desk Program which endeavored to support all aspects of community life, skills, and development for women within the church. My father passed away from a serious illness when I was five, and my mother was my guide and the center of my universe. She was formidable in her energy, and integrity, uncompromising in expectations, and the first person to teach me the importance of confidence.

I was taught to set personal standards and boundaries, be accountable and strive to do my best in all situations. I knew what was expected of me. It was a challenge to live up to this epitome of virtue and accomplishment, who was able to love and accept the realities and challenges life had thrown her way. She was and will always be my role model. She gave me the confidence to strive for dreams undefined and aspirations seemingly out of reach. My foundation was established in confidence, and my expectations and dreams were set high.

My personal journey in confidence began in grade school in Ghana. In sixth grade, I became the school Prefect. This was a great honor. My mother was proud of me, and I was proud of myself. I had meaningful responsibilities, I had a modicum of respect and authority, and I was part of a decision-making team. I joined teacher-student meetings and planned activities for the students. I was a trusted courier of documents.

In our Friday morning general assemblies, I assisted the teachers with health checks. We checked hair for creepy crawlies, teeth for oral care, and fingernails for cleanliness. I loved writing the health-check report notes to parents. When the students carried home their health check reports, they often got into trouble for bringing home a note that indicated a deficiency. Then I became the scapegoat. I lost friends, called a snitch and teachers' pet. I was ostracized. With buckets of tears, I sat alone at lunch. I suffered agonizing loneliness and my confidence wavered. Finally, I talked to my mother about the situation.

"Why is the health inspection important to do?" Mom queried.

"My teacher says it helps to keep the students from becoming sick and having to go to the hospital and the dentist."

"So do you think it is important to continue to do this, even though your friends are upset with you?"

"Yes Mother."

I recognized that I could not shirk my responsibility simply because it caused me discomfort. Mom reminded me of a Ghanaian proverb that states "It is easy to break one stalk of a raffia broom, but almost impossible to break a whole broom unless one applies a machete to cut it." The lesson was clear—I needed the support of my friends to weather the storm, for strength in numbers and the collective energy of the group, and to conjure the magic of togetherness.

I was confident in my task and in my approach to ending my loneliness. I talked to my best school friend about it. She offered to help me talk with the other children during playtime. We started by organizing a small army of close friends—a strike force, purposeful, intentional, focused and armed with the relevant information. We got together at playtime over my mom's homemade orange scones—an irresistible treat specially made for the occasion. One might be tempted to call it a bribe, though I prefer to think of it as the honey that drew the bees. While eating our scones, I explained why the health checks were important. Surprisingly some of them shared quick understanding, and had stories to share like "My mother told me if I have dirt in my nails, and I eat with my hands I will get sick, and I can have worms in my tummy which will come out of my bottom." The other children were horrified, the story spread like wildfire, handwashing became a popular activity, and children wanted their nails trimmed.

We had cemented a fundamental truth, that there was value in doing the health checks and sending notes home to parents, which helped with care that prevented worms from living in stomachs and crawling out of bottoms! Slowly others came around and played with me. Life got better.

The raffia broom lesson stayed with me, and I suggested to the teachers to have additional students assist with health checks on Fridays. To be nominated as a health checker was a prestigious goal for students and the criteria was tied to good behavior, to high scores in mental math, to the best essay of the week, and to the best handwriting. Once there were multiple health checkers, we divided the student population into four groups: reds, yellows, greens, and blues. We created a game which made the activity competitive and fun. Whichever group had the lowest number of health notes won a treat.

My small army of friends had become change agents, implicitly recognized as the go-to students. We started helping children with schoolwork. This led to my first endeavor. I established a homework club, in Mom's garage, where my friends and I tutored children after school and got paid in treats. My earliest experiences of strategic problem-solving. lessons in leadership, followership, influencing, and confidence building happened because I did not walk away at the first sign of perceived failure. My initial lessons in confidence building were surprisingly concrete given my age. I learned:

- Do not walk away from difficult situations, it's better to apply creative solutions.

- Be open to the input and the support of others—build community.
- The broom is stronger and more indestructible than the single raffia stalk.
- The *why* matters.
- It is possible to change others' understanding using a thoughtful planned approach.

I gained confidence from being a health checker and from my friends' responses. I learned to not give up easily and to act well in difficult times. Of course, I did not fully appreciate the complexity of the principles and experiences at that time, but in reflection I see their power. My role also taught me that leadership can be lonely and stressful. However, if I believed in the assignment, then I could work with others to achieve group goals. My first layer of confidence development had begun. It would build over time into the existential framework that supports the whole of me at this time in my life.

Seventh grade found me in an all-girls boarding school, the beginning of the next seven years of my life. The transition was exciting for me—freedom from home, and independence in managing my own time and affairs. The possibilities seemed endless and highly promising. The reality was overwhelming and confusing. Finding my path to confidence was a challenge. There were lots more students. I was lost in the crowd, nameless, faceless, and with no identity to which I could cleave.

In this new community, I did not have a clan, a lineage with roots to hold me down, or a clear role that made sense of this new chaotic world. I realized that my upbringing was unique, and I had to change my approach to making friends. Changing gears required an attitude change, openness to others' views and experiences, learning to be non-judgmental, and learning to transition from my prior leadership role to being a member of a group with no special role.

In retrospect, it was an opportunity to learn about myself, to develop a new level of awareness of engagement with others, to survive in different environments, and to build endurance and perseverance, while growing my ability to compete at all levels. Having been in a leading role during grade school, it was disorienting to find myself in a position where I was a part of the pack, with no special role or distinguishing qualities—a novice, unremarkable, part of a grey wallpaper backdrop, barely existent, and missing my specific identity.

Feeling lost and invisible I disappeared into a fantasy world of books. I read voraciously and became Alice in Wonderland, Peter Pan, Kwaku Anansi, and any character that would help me gain an identity and become visible. I dove into the English classics—Chaucer, Donne, Shakespeare, and oh the wonderful confusion of reading *Lady Chatterley's Lover* as a seventh grader and being reported to the house mistress for reading a highly inappropriate book! Dear Lord—what a to-do that caused. Mom was summoned to the school where she had to confess I got the book out of her personal library.

The English literature teacher was assigned to supervise my reading, and my imagination exploded with new sights, sounds, colors, and textures. It was blissful. I discovered curiosity, a doorway into worlds unknown, mystical, inexplicable, and altogether joyous. My next layer of confidence began to build, based on discovering that curiosity could be a catalyst for transformation and growth. I learned:

- Curiosity can facilitate learning.
- Knowledge can be gained from different dimensions of exposure.
- All learning is valuable—structured, experiential, or inadvertent.

After seven years in boarding school, having attained my "0" and "A" levels, with great excitement I transitioned to the university for my baccalaureate nursing program. Oh, I felt so grown up—my own semi-private room, total independence, a social life; what was not to like? I had a busy academic schedule, and mountains of new knowledge that started off confusing, disconnected, overwhelming, and downright daunting at times. Nursing school was both challenging and delightful.

The first year of learning seemed disjointed and not useful until I started my clinical experiences, and then it all fell into place. Praxis was transformative. I was confident and filled with the purpose of caring for patients, working with others, creating change, and seeing concrete results. Some days and experiences were terrifying, others sad. There were patients that I could not make better the way I had hoped, and sometimes patients died. As a young nursing student, their deaths seemed to me indiscriminate and senseless. I recall my shock and fear as a midwife-in-training and delivering babies for women who had never accessed antenatal care during their pregnancy.

One patient wasn't aware she was carrying twins. As I admitted her into the labor ward and examined her, I was stunned to assess several extremities indicating more than one baby. Fear kicked in. Was I skilled enough to help this patient safely deliver her babies? What if I made a mistake? Panicked thoughts raced through my brain. I looked into her fearful eyes, and inside I felt my focus shift.

A deep certainty settled in my gut, knowing within that I was able and prepared for the task. With a firm voice and a reassuring smile, I spoke her name and held her hand, and the worry eased from her eyes. We worked together to get those two babies out safely. Together, she and I delivered a miracle. I graduated with a bachelor's in nursing and psychology, with specialties in midwifery, mental health, and public health. I found my connection to purpose. I am a service to others. I learned:

- Knowledge, skill, and confidence develop over time.
- Experiencing joy in my work energized me and transformed my performance and confidence.
- Knowledge and skill development came with an exciting journey of surprising discoveries.

I completed my national service in Ghana after graduating from nursing school. Then I set my sights on England. Mom, my long-term role model, had been a student at the University of Cambridge, and I wanted to follow in her footsteps and share her journey. It was the beginning of my independent adult life, a new journey in finding and developing my identity and confidence.

The challenges were seemingly limitless—the language, the environment of care, different and unfamiliar equipment, care delivery approaches, and the cold, wet British weather. The move was the biggest challenge I had yet faced, and for the first time in my life I was surprised to experience overt and covert racism.

Racism ranged from patients requesting different staff to care for them to teammates stating they didn't want to work with me because of my accent. I had two options—develop the skills to adapt and flourish in that situation or step away from my chosen career.

On a personal level, I was starting a family, and this shifted my priorities. I had a partner and children to fold into my choices and decision-making. I chose to lean in and develop my professional skills and rise above the racial undertones. I gathered the internal strength to persevere through the challenges. I generated the patience to acculturate and gave myself the opportunity to thrive.

My career in England started in acute care, and then I transitioned to post-acute care and mental health. My collective professional experiences created an urgency to expand my skills, and I decided to further my education. I chose an innovative inaugural Master of Science program focused on primary care in a context of inter-agency, intersectoral, and interprofessional collaborative practice. My learnings in this program became the bedrock of my advanced practice, opening doors for me to work confidently in diverse settings.

The beginning semester required participation in a one-week program within a psychotherapeutic setting where students learned about their professional selves. We learned how we each were perceived, our communication styles, and how we function on an interdisciplinary team. I learned characteristics about myself that at the time I only vaguely understood.

I was not aware of how I projected myself in professional settings. The feedback I received during this experience was consistent with learnings from my childhood experiences in leading. I was characterized as a change maker, focused on addressing challenges; analytical, collaborative, and connected to purpose and attainment of tangible results. A fascinating facet of my personality that became evident during this process was that problem-solving was an inherent characteristic for me.

In today's professional world, I would be identified as a disrupter. In my professional settings, I ascended the proverbial corporate ladder against a backdrop of varied and sometimes indescribable, unexpected, and baffling experiences. I was told it was inappropriate to wear my traditional Ghanaian fabric corporate suits to work. My naturally black hair presented problems in work settings. And my ever-present accent seemed noticeable even in silence.

Striving to belong, to fit, to be acknowledged for my contributions, to be me—the hurt could be overwhelming. To be judged and identified by my clothing, hair, and speech and not be given agency because of my capabilities was distressing. To be purposefully separated from my unique identity, rooted in my lineage, my clan, and my native community was counter to my culture and upbringing. I was surrounded by people with no clan, no roots, and no community as part of their identity.

I was often disoriented, empty, and lacking my bearing. Perseverance, focus, determination, and sheer grit saw me through. I was committed to my survival and progress. I got up each day, put one foot in front of the other, and reached for my goals despite, or because of, my belittling surroundings. I learned:

- Confidence development is multifactorial and builds from within.
- One grows from pain in unexpected ways.

- Intentionally taking time to reflect on one's experiences is essential for growth and development.

Having worked and studied in England for over fourteen years, I became curious about how other healthcare systems functioned. Whimsically, I also thought that having obtained my baccalaureate education in Ghana, and my master's education in England, it would be the perfect professional trifecta if I obtained my doctoral education in the United States. Besides, Mom had graduated from Cornell University in Ithaca, so why not follow in her footsteps again?

Armed with the confidence of years of diverse clinical, leadership, and educational practice and skills, I relocated to the United States. The challenges of the move to England paled in comparison to the shock of moving to the United States. To start with, they drove on the opposite side of the road. They super-sized everything. They spoke an indecipherable American slang, lived a regionally geographic culture, and followed a completely different way of life. And the clinical practice environment was also entirely new.

Everything from care delivery to funding models to medical nomenclature did not match any of my previous experience. This was a new Everest to climb. Again, I faced the choice of pulling up my socks and reaching for aspirational new goals or abandoning my dreams and settling for what was known and comfortable.

I leaned into my confidence and by now deep knowledge of self to commence this journey. I moved forward with determination, passed my nursing board exam, and immersed myself in learning. Given my love of teaching, I pursued a post-master's nurse-educator program, and on completion of the program, transitioned into and completed a doctorate in nursing practice.

Foundational to this journey, the intrinsic motivation that sustained me, the energy and purpose that drove me was my embedded knowledge of my unique identity, rooted in my lineage, my clan, and my native community. The expectations aligned with my identity and belongingness are a visceral knowing within, a palpable reminder of my very existence. So where is Praba, daughter of Hannah Victoria Koomson and the ancestral grandchild child of the Reverend Pra Koomson?

As I write to you, dear reader, I live in the United States and am employed with a large integrated healthcare system. I do work that utilizes my diverse body of skills, knowledge, and passion for healthcare and education. I develop curriculum and teach at the master's and doctoral levels in nursing in academic nursing institutions, as well as in clinical settings. I speak nationally and internationally on healthcare issues and publish my academic and practice work.

Most recently, I set up The HanVick Foundation in honor of Mom, my beloved mentor and role model, community advocate, and champion of others. The foundation is a nonprofit organization dedicated to providing mentoring and education on the care of elders in the community, and support for caregivers. Over the course of my life, my ability to achieve my goals and aspirations has been built on the confidence I developed through knowledge of my unique identity, lineage, clan, and connection to the community. Reader, I share with you my confidence framework, in hopes that it may be of value to you as you make your own journey.

1. Know your identity—irrefutably.
2. Know what gives you energy and joy in your life and aspirations.
3. Connect to purpose within diverse settings with intent and a desire to be your best.
4. Focus on what matters most—your personal values, choices, and preferences.
5. Set your personal standards so others don't set them for you.
6. Live your dreams and aspirations and be present for yourself.
7. Recognize your achievements and failures and reach for your best, not perfection.
8. Celebrate yourself and maintain your intrinsic motivation to be what you want to be.
9. Be your authentic self.

CONFIDENCE FRAMEWORK

Know your identity—irrefutably.	Who am I? Where and to whom do I belong?
Know what gives you energy and joy in your life and aspirations.	What am I passionate about? What do I want? What fills me up? Where do I draw strength and inspiration from?
Connect to purpose within diverse settings with intent and a desire to be your best.	Where am I? Who is here with me? What are we doing here? How do we do it best? What should I strive to contribute?
Focus on what matters most—your personal values, choices, and preferences.	What is important to me? What will I not compromise? What do I strive towards?
Set your personal standards so others don't set them for you.	What is important to me? What will I not do as a matter of principle?
Live your dreams and aspirations and be present for yourself.	What is my dream? How do I connect to it daily? How does it drive what I do? How will I know when I have my dream?
Recognize your achievements and failures and reach for your best, not perfection.	What have I done excellently and to the best of my ability? What can I do better?

Celebrate yourself and maintain your intrinsic motivation to be what you want to be.	How do I see myself?
Be your authentic self.	Who am I? What am I? Where am I on my journey?

Sankofa is a Ghanaian tradition that encourages one to include the past in the present. As the daughter of Hannah Victoria Koomson, I am an educator and a force for good in the communities in which I move. As the ancestral grandchild of Pra, I too am a healer, serving my clan and my community.

I am Praba Koomson. I am the daughter of Hannah Victoria Koomson and the ancestral grandchild child of the Reverend Pra Koomson. This is my core uniqueness, who I am, where I am from, the foundational mapping of my lineage, and the community of people with whom I belong. My identity, my roots, my lineage, my clan, and the intersectionality of these four elements provide the framework of my being.

INTRODUCING DR. BELINDA HYPPOLITE

Dr. Belinda Higgs Hyppolite is an empathetic leader, entrepreneur, builder, cultivator, innovator, and creator. She has taken on increasing roles of responsibility over twenty-seven years in higher education. Dr. Higgs Hyppolite's career is focused on social justice issues plaguing faculty, staff, students, and communities. She is committed to advancing access, belonging, inclusion, and social justice in higher education. Dr. Higgs Hyppolite has supported and advocated for marginalized student populations: low-income, first generation, foster care, in public and private schools, Deferred Action for Childhood Arrivals (DACA), and for students, veterans, and homeless students in Temporary Protective Status. She facilitates teaching circles and symposiums to promote universal design and more inclusive classroom spaces. She serves as a mentor to many but has a strong affinity to serving and guiding female leaders.

Throughout her career, Dr. Higgs Hyppolite advocated for the voiceless through her work in diversity education and oppression reduction. As a social justice advocate and educator, she believes that access to education is a right, not a privilege. Persevering in her journey to promote the success of diverse faculty, staff, and students, Dr. Hyppolite is proud to serve as the Vice President and Chief Diversity Officer at the University of Oklahoma. She is the wife to James Hyppolite and the proud mother to Sarah, Brandon, Zahara, and one fur baby, Pepper.

YOU ARE MORE

You are bigger than your emotions, your job titles, the positions you hold, and your salaries. You can be and become whatever you desire. Achieving your dreams requires hard work and full accountability. Anything you want to be or do, can be done. I speak from my experiences as an accomplished Black female leader. I am educated and have a lot of letters behind my name. And still the alphabet soup and the twenty-seven years of professional experience do not define me. I charted a course to drive my success. I worked hard to avoid being perceived in the negative stereotypes Black women are assigned and disparaged in American culture.

I engage in the extra labor of entering spaces with a smile, and I am keenly aware of my tone and presence. I squelch my emotions to prevent being perceived as aggressive or angry, even when those emotions are warranted. Striving to overcome the barriers of stereotyping, bias, labeling, shunning, unfair comparisons, lack of recognition, lower salaries, and feeling inferior is exhausting. You must learn to advocate for yourself and embrace the nuances that make you a unique human being. Learning lessons in confidence is a lifelong journey, starting with admitting your current confidence level, being intentional about your desired outcomes, and defining your success; then going after it.

I am a proud wife, mother, and a C-suite executive. I am a recognized leader in my industry. I strive to be a supportive, transformational, and inspirational leader. I overcame adversity and worked hard to make and leave a positive impact wherever I went. Even with my accomplishments I am still uncomfortable with accolades. It is important to realize that the person you see as a confident leader may have a different internal reality and still may be endeavoring to secure her confidence.

Throughout my life there were real periods of struggle and bouts of low self-esteem and confidence. Guess what? The people around me had no idea what I was experiencing internally. Outwardly, I was a beacon of light, strong, with unwavering confidence; no one knew my internal dialogue that told me I was not good enough. I, like many women, created a character that allowed me to show up and face the day. I leaned into this character to meet the challenges and daunting tasks that lay ahead. I gave voice and power to people that did not deserve my time and attention. I overanalyzed almost everything, destroying my enjoyment, and exhausting my mental stores. I am a remarkable woman and powerful female leader, but I am still learning and leaning into my confidence journey. I am gaining confidence because I have a purpose and destiny to fulfill. I am—we are—bigger than our emotions, job titles, positions at work or home, or salaries.

I am the third child of five daughters born to Harley and Rae Higgs. I grew up in a small town in the bootheel of Missouri and come from a lineage of strong, beautiful, talented women. We are known for creating gourmet meals out of discarded scraps and building churches from abandoned bricks. We overcame obstacles and adversity by fostering relationships and bridges with an array of peoples. We never let our race, economic status, location, educational levels, or naysayers distract us from achieving what seemed impossible. Our byword was, "If you can conceive it, then you can achieve it." This beautiful tapestry of strength and resilience is the foundation upon which I built my life and my dreams. Harley, my father, is a Pastor, so a relationship with God and spirituality were central to my upbringing. The formula we embodied was Christ + Education = Success.

Each of us are on our own path, and my family's version of Christ or spirituality is not required for success, nonetheless this was the formula I worked from to construct my life and my confidence.

As a younger woman, I struggled to find my spot and voice; being the third of five children, it was easy to go unnoticed. Watching my siblings, I learned what to do and not do. I became good at people-pleasing and knowing when to be seen and heard. I wanted my parents to be proud, my friends to like and accept me, and I wanted my teachers to see me for myself and not compare me to my older siblings. I worked hard in school, extracurricular activities, and in the church. I was committed to being the best and strove to add value to each environment. I helped others even though I was still figuring things out myself.

Both my older sisters were amazing seamstresses, they loved fabrics and fashion, they could look at a pattern and reproduce the cover in real time. I didn't want to take Home Economics class but was interested in taking Wood Shop and wanted to build things. I was encouraged to follow in my sisters' footsteps because they were both so gifted, so surely, I would have the same success and passion. I did not! Although I performed well in the class—I laid out fabrics, pinned patterns to fabric, and measured ingredients to produce the perfect batch of cookies—I absolutely hated every minute of it. Threading the sewing machine was impossible. Following a recipe was boring. It would have been great to explore my own passion, but instead, I plodded the path assigned to me, even when I did not enjoy it or know why I followed it. I did not know who I was or how to advocate for myself and my interests. I lived by the external set of rules explained to me. I had not yet taken ownership or accountability for my life. I carried this habit and approach with me into higher education and nearly beyond.

I had two undergraduate degrees and was about to start law school when I realized I had no idea what I was doing, where my life was headed, or even who I was. I worked to get into law school, took the test, secured the scholarship, and prepared to commence schooling. I had no confidence or ideas about my future. Upon my acceptance I started the first semester in a prestigious law school. I was doing it. I was months into the semester faking my confidence, faking my desires, and I cried myself to sleep every night. I wanted to make my parents proud, but I was miserable. I followed a course that had been mapped for me. I dotted the I's and crossed the T's and marched forward on my assigned journey, never truly engaging in the process, pushing back for my own interests, or being accountable for the quality and enjoyment of my life. Everyone else thought my law degree would guarantee a successful and happy life.

During my tear-filled nights I realized I had given others agency over my life. I was suffering and I came to understand that I had to chart my own course. I had to take ownership of who I was, where I was going, and what I was going to be. This was the first step towards real confidence building for me: ownership. I required ownership of my life, my success, and my dreams for me to build my confidence. It is a wakeup call when you realize you are living out someone else's plans, someone else's dreams. And it takes courage to admit this to yourself, but it is an excellent first step. Own your life. Own your identity now and determine your future identity. Other people cannot live your life, you must learn to navigate it yourself. Learning to do what is best for yourself without apology is critical when taking ownership of your life. It also means you are taking accountability for the outcomes, either good or bad.

One Sunday afternoon I called my parents. I had not discussed my decision with my sisters, and we usually talked about everything. With shaking hands, I dialed my parents' number.

"Hello?" The clear voice of my mama rang through the wires.

"Mama," I took a deep breath and plunged on. "I have to tell you something."

I paused again and I heard her breath catch.

"Everything is alright. I am fine. I am fine." I stammered. "But I have decided to leave law school."

I had planned and discussed my career with advisors and professors. They helped me chart a new path for myself, so I was not completely unprepared for this conversation. I told her I was going out of state to pursue a new career and educational opportunity. To my relief she was accepting and happy for me, but she also put me on notice that I would have to share the news with daddy on my own. She would not tell him for me. Accountability. Ownership. I had to stand up and tell the person who had designed my path, that I was stepping off that path and forging my own, new one.

I dropped out of law school. I took my life in a different direction. It was scary. I had already engaged in several conversations with my faculty advisor and received great advice. I had done prep work and felt like I had a solid plan moving forward. The wheels were in motion, I was taking my life in a new direction. I had to face my fears, because, at the end of the day, this was a decision that I had to live with.

Doubt and fear threatened to stifle me, but I pressed

on. I questioned if I was doing the right thing. I prayed for direction and toiled many nights trying to ensure I had thought of all the scenarios for what would come next. The advice I received remained similar: it's your life, and you must do what is best for you. I wasn't sure if I had received a clear direction from God, but the decision was made, I was leaving law school. I did not want to go back home, so I sorted out my next move and how I would push forward. I activated a plan that I unknowingly set in motion before I entered law school. I knew I wanted to pursue further education, remembering our equation Christ + Education = Success. I had the Christ part down and was continuing to work on the Education part of the formula.

Then my negative self-talk took over. I beat myself up, second-guessed myself, and over analyzed everything. I created doom and gloom scenarios of things not working out, and my "what if's" took center stage and threatened to paralyze my actions. I did not have it all sorted or decided, but leading confidently is not about having all the right answers or seeing a clearly mapped path. Leading with confidence is learning to trust yourself and having faith in your plan, knowing the desired outcome can be achieved.

I moved to the Quad-Cities (the mid-border area of

Iowa-Illinois) and accepted a job at a small private liberal arts college. I was enrolled and was accepted into a master's program. I felt proud but I was equally terrified. In retrospect, deciding to leave law school and go to graduate school led to an amazing career, in which I have traveled the globe and created a life of clarity and abundance. I met my best friend, became a godparent, experienced love, and loss, and learned a bit more about myself each day. I learned that you could take a risk and reap a harvest of blessings. I was courageous enough to make bold moves while being wildly uncomfortable. The greatest growth occurs when humans are outside of their comfort zones. I did not let fear guide my decisions, and if I had, I would not be where I am today.

Now I am at a new level, personally and professionally. These experiences shaped the confident woman I am. My definition of confidence continues to evolve, but there are a few characteristics that are salient to my identity; being comfortable living in my skin, learning to honor my imperfections, and having harmony in my life. I am not sure what balance is or if it can be achieved, but I strive for excellence even as perfection is elusive and embrace my culture and identity as a Black woman living in America. Society has a lot to say about who I should be and what I should do.

I do not have to convince anyone of my value or worth, and it takes courage and confidence to embrace this fact. I show up and demonstrate my professionalism. Confidence is getting the privilege to be yourself every day. As women, we do not have to surrender to our struggles, anxiety, depression, self-doubt, or disappointments. Sometimes we must learn new skills to help us overcome barriers that keep us stuck and cause our confidence to wane. Every life experience is an opportunity to boost and grow our confidence. Lean into doing the work, and your confidence will grow.

In retrospect I can see the steps I took to build my confidence and now I proudly share them with you.

Lesson #1: Ownership

Take ownership of your life, your identity, your dreams, and your future. As I shared above, I people-pleased myself out of existence and agency. I gave my power to others and sometimes gave their opinions more value than my own lived experiences.

To take ownership means you act or possess your feelings, emotions, and actions. Your behavior does not depend on what others are saying or doing. Many women have been conditioned to let others decide for them. Ownership means you make your own decisions and live with the consequences. This doesn't mean you shouldn't take advice from those that you trust, but it does mean that when you decide, then you accept the consequences, both good and bad.

Lesson #2: Silence the negative voices in your head.
Life is full of ups and downs, twists and turns, positives, and negatives. This is your journey and you do not need anyone's approval to make your best decisions. When self-doubt creeps in and you start to question if you can achieve a new goal, be willing to tell yourself *Yes! I can do this!* Invest in yourself and silence those voices within that keep you from moving forward. Overcoming negative thoughts takes effort, same as learning any new skill.

The first step is identifying your negative self-talk. Sometimes we do not even realize we are beating ourselves up. After you identify it, there are tools and techniques you can deploy to stop negative self-talk. My method of eliminating negative thoughts was to focus on the things that brought me joy and helped me advance my goals. I decided I was stronger than my negative self-talk and was going to be a beacon of light. I created a mental picture in my mind of who I was and what I was going to be. A mentor told me, "You cannot pour from an empty cup." I filled my cup with joy and confidence. I silenced my negative self-talk by giving it no purchase, no room in my mind, or in my life. I am a source of power and light. You are too. I am not the failure I told myself I was.

Lesson #3: Be willing to step out.
Willingness shows up differently for each person. If you never take a step forward or try something new, how do you know if you can do it? Many successes throughout my career came because I was willing to try. I took the risk and said yes. Willingness does not mean I enter a situation blindly, but I am open to do something different, to move to a new location, or take on a new role to see the outcome.

Being willing does not mean you will succeed, but a failure is an event, not a person. Successful people have more failures in their rearview than unsuccessful people because they were willing to take the chance. Willingness can take you to places and unveil ideas that doubt cannot see. Fear and doubt will shroud and limit who you are and what you can be. Do not make decisions out of fear. Willingness is a combination of trusting the head and honoring the heart. Be willing—and remember that failures position you for new learnings. When you are willing to step into new challenges your confidence grows. Be willing.

Lesson #4: Be humble and courageous.

Courage and humility are not often grouped together, but they complement each other. Humility is a sign of strength. To be a humble leader, you must be self-aware and confident in who you are and how you add value. Humility is about your inner peace and outward attitude; inner peace is not a spirit of arrogance or pridefulness, but a calming confident spirit that reminds you of who you are and why you operate the way you do. Humility is a quiet strength. Courage means you are willing, have silenced the voices in your head, and are not bending to your fears but are using the doubts as a launching pad to move forward on your journey.

Real courage, and lots of it, is required to progress on your confidence-building journey. It is easy to look at others and believe they are winning, achieving all their goals, and living perfect lives. My Pastor once said, "It is nice to notice how green the neighbor's grass is, but did you ever consider the cost of their water bill?" Success and excellence often come at a cost. Are you willing to pay the cost? Leading confidently involves giving, constructing, and communicating with people. Confident leaders manage processes, people, and emotions while actively listening and then driving results. It takes courage to lead, bring about improvements, and leverage obstacles as opportunities. It takes courage to be your authentic self and to be vulnerable.

What do you need to grow and build your confidence? Courage. Its acronym has worked wonders for my confidence building.

Confidence = Courage—C. O. U. R. A. G. E.

C = Create space for failure and explore new possibilities.

O = Open your heart to new opportunities and new experiences.

U = Understand your purpose and embrace that you are an original.

R = Respect yourself and respect others.

A = Ask questions to increase your knowledge and understanding.

G = Grow in grace and remain grounded in your values.

E = Encourage yourself and others.

Being confident does not mean you are the loudest, always the first to speak, or working a room with poise and precision. Having a grounding, confident presence serves to reassure others and allows others to be their authentic selves.

C = **Create space for failure and explore new possibilities.**
Creating space is about giving yourself permission to not be perfect but striving to improve. Failure is a valuable lesson because it is a steppingstone for improvement. Use failure to shape your future choices. Moments of disappointment birth new opportunities for improvement and growth. Most women are comfortable extending grace and empathy to others, but when it comes to self-love, acceptance, and appreciation, we deem ourselves unworthy. Many women honor their struggles through harsh criticism, constant reminders, and overindulgence in self-pity. These strategies might work for a while, but they will not help build your confidence or lead to enlightenment. Learn to accept failure and then create a space for recovery and new discoveries.

O = **Open your heart to new opportunities and new experiences.**
It is easier to receive when we have open hands and hearts. When we are closed to receiving feedback, constructive criticism, and guidance, we close ourselves from learning and improving. Closed minds lead to missed opportunities and experiences. Those who already know everything leave no room to learn or to receive anything new. Are you that person? Do you become defensive and

feel the need to provide justification for yourself or your work, or do you take a moment to listen and ponder on what is being shared? These probing questions help gauge where you are on the openness scale.

When you are confident in your skills and abilities, you understand that a feedback loop is part of development. When you are closed, you miss opportunities and experiences. According to the Oxford Dictionary (2022), fear is an emotion that resides in our head but is not grounded in reality; it occupies space in our brain or subconscious. Being open and remaining open requires action. One must make intentional efforts, stay persistent against fear and doubt, and do not give it purchase lest it creep back into your decision making. Create a mental picture of who you are and what you want to be, then speak it into existence. As a person speaks or believes, so it shall be. We must speak life into ourselves and others. Be brave and lean into your confidence.

U = Understand your purpose and embrace that you are an original.

Understanding one's purpose can be a lifelong target. Comparison politics cultivate conditions that breed doubt, are riddled with pitfalls, and are counter to productivity. As women, we must bury the cycle of comparing ourselves to others. Living your best life means you understand that another individual cannot fulfill your assignment nor have your impact. If it is your assignment, only you can achieve the results. If you did not get the job, then it was not your job. If you did not get the acceptance letter, it was not where you were supposed to be. This way of thinking might be new and even challenging but know that no one else can receive the life that is designed for you.

There is a reason each of us is on this earth, and when we embrace self-discovery, we are better positioned to fulfill our purpose and share our unique and special gifts. Purpose means you have an immediate and longer-term strategy for success. Why does this matter? If you do not have a clear purpose and plan, you impact your ability to lead with confidence. Harley often proclaimed, "If you aim at nothing, you will hit it every time."

A purpose and goal provide clarity and guideposts when courage or confidence is lacking. We are building our confidence muscles. The more you use your confidence muscles, the more defined and stronger you become. If you do not use your confidence muscles, they atrophy, weaken, or degenerate. Developing a plan for your life with specific markers and desired outcomes is a great place to start; they serve you well when your confidence flags.

R = Respect yourself and respect others.
Historically, America has not demonstrated respect or deference towards women or people of color. It was not until 1920 when congress ratified the 19th amendment, fully giving women the right to vote. The Civil Rights Act of 1964 took another forty years. Learning to respect yourself and others should be a simple ask and expectation, but we live in a divided world with divided communities, churches, and schools. Historic harms have resurfaced, and we are again facing the things we thought America had overcome.

We do not live in a post-racial country, and the sins of the past are now the sins of the present. Social injustices and unrest are on display on TV, social media, and in our communities. Issues surrounding race and racism continue to be the unfinished business of America and the world.

We must learn to embrace people for who they are and build more inclusive communities. Respect does not mean validation or agreement with another person's values or life choices. Respect means honoring your ability to live a full life with your own choices. Respect is wrapped in skills, such as being able to challenge one's own assumptions, actively listening to different perspectives and points of view, remaining flexible and agile because there are multiple correct answers to life's challenges, and apologizing when you learn you harmed someone, whether it was intentional or unintentional.

You cannot respect others if you do not love and respect yourself. You must overcome societal pressures and identities assigned to you, then build your confidence on the foundation of respecting and loving yourself. You grow to know your value and your worth. Be unapologetic about who you are and stop trying to live up to others' expectations. Respecting yourself means you are actively working to honor the things that bring you joy and discard the things that keep you in bondage.

Many are living in self-created prisons of other's expectations or societal identities. Melinda French Gates said, "Women need to remember to set an agenda, or someone else will." Respecting and loving who you are is a foundational component to confidence building.

A = Ask questions to increase your knowledge and understanding.

There is pressure to always have the answer or to provide an appropriate response. Asking questions is essential to confidence because it demonstrates a commitment to learning. Making assumptions or jumping into a situation without context creates a greater likelihood of harm and error. Asking questions shows vulnerability and curiosity.

Curiosity is a great launch point for courage and confidence. This deliberate act of asking and listening to the response leads to joint innovation and creativity. Knowledge is power. We often miss the acquisition phase of developing and gaining knowledge. If you want to be impactful, to be a leader, and to be a futurist, you must ask questions. The strongest relationships are often forged through the exchange of information and experiences. Our stories reveal who we are and provide a snapshot of what we have endured. Asking questions is an action that generates positive results and confidence building.

G = Grow in grace and remain grounded in your values. Showing grace and empathy for others is not an emotion we have been conditioned to extend willfully. In fact, it took several pandemics (e.g., COVID, social unrest, and political polarization) to help normalize the words empathy, grace, and patience. While locked in our homes, we needed a reminder to extend grace. Grace is our ability to forgive and accept the things we cannot control. Whether that forgiveness is towards us or others, we all stand in need.

Courage and confidence complement each other because it is hard to attain confidence without courage. I easily forgive my children, spouse, and employees for making mistakes or failing to meet expectations. However, when it comes to forgiving myself, I struggle. I often play the movie reel of past mistakes in my head, reminding myself of past errors. Growing in grace is an iterative and continuing process that I am still working on. We must extend the grace to ourselves that we so willingly extend to others. Giving yourself grace takes courage and builds your confidence.

E = Encourage yourself and others.

I am a preacher's child; and growing up in the church, music played, and continues to play, an enormous role in bringing communities together. Donald Lawrence (2006) is a gospel icon who wrote a song entitled, *Encourage Yourself.* The lyrics focus on overcoming obstacles, criticisms, enemies, mistakes, disappointment, and challenges. The song addresses self-doubt, the loss of hope, and the desire to give up when life becomes difficult to manage. The theme throughout the song stresses the importance of encouraging yourself and speaking life into your dark moments. Encouragement is giving support or hope to yourself or to someone else. Support comes through words, actions, gifts, and even through song. When you encourage yourself, you give yourself permission to go in a different direction, to course-correct and to accept a new adventure, or to try something new.

Living life fully creates times of doubt or disbelief; there are instances where we have lost hope, there is no way forward, and we will not succeed. No matter what happens, if you are not dead, there is still something you can do. While on your path to success, learn to enjoy the journey, trust the process, and recover when you stumble and fall.

There is a significant difference between our comfort zones and our growth zones. The territory in the middle of these two zones is where knowledge, development, and confidence-building occur. Positions are temporary; health fades, and titles can be stripped. All lives have equal value, but not all lives have equal access. Your beginning might have been rough, and your middle labored with bumps and bruises, but your destination is yet to come.

Confidence is finding and using your voice to impact positive change. Self-confidence is not something you achieve, and you get to check the *I have confidence* box. It is a skill that requires routine cultivation and attention. Confidence building is not linear; it might take circuitous routes and consistent focus to build.

My confidence building journey started when I took ownership of my life. After that I had to focus on eliminating my negative self-talk, on being open to new opportunities, and on the idea of failing—embracing my humility and building my courage.

Your confidence journey may have started by embracing your courage. Any which way you get there, or do it, keep your focus on improving and bolstering your confidence. Use goals and priorities as guideposts and buoys to sustain you through periods of low confidence. Whenever you feel weak and your spirit is shaken, remember the season you are in will not last forever. Life provides many occasions for courage and confidence to be revealed.

Confidence is magnetic and can attract distractions. Be aware of people and things that come to derail your focus. Light and darkness cannot exist in the same space. Your confidence must be grounded in truth and clarity. You are not responsible for convincing someone that you have value and worth. However, you are responsible for your happiness and your life. You are the chief executive officer of your life, and how you respond to difficult situations is to display your confidence. We each have a voice and unique talents; use your sphere of influence to build a bridge, open a door, or decrease a barrier for others.

You are more than your emotions, your job title, and your salary. You can be and become whatever you want to be. Do not let others define your success. Take ownership, and lead confidently.

INTRODUCING DR. CINDY GIRMAN

Cindy is Founder and President of CERobs Consulting, LLC, with thirty consultants under contract and over fifty pharmaceutical company clients. Dr. Cindy Girman is an industry-leading pharmacoepidemiology expert in real world evidence and clinical outcomes. Her forty-plus year career focuses on clinical trial and observational study design and analytic methods, particularly using electronic health records or insurance claims. She helps clients with endpoint strategies for trials by identifying outcomes that are meaningful to and resonate with patients.

Cindy is fervently interested in addiction treatments and research, having lost a son due to accidental overdose. She is funding and collaborating with researchers on a new promising non-pharmacological treatment. Except for administrative costs, proceeds from her first book,

A Voice from Heaven, launching in 2024, will be donated to research on addiction. She and her husband Tom have established pharmacoepidemiology scholarships at the University of North Carolina.

Cindy holds a Doctorate in Public Health in Biostatistics from the University of North Carolina, and a Master of Science in Applied Statistics-Computer Science from Villanova University. She splits her time between the coast and mountains of North Carolina, where she hones her writing skills and practices spiritual growth. Cindy is proud of her daughter, Vera, a professional fashion photographer. Cindy enjoys spending time with family and friends as well as taking safari and exotic birding trips with her life partner, friend, and husband, Tom.

ANXIOUS OVER-ACHIEVER

3:15 am, sometime in October 2014

I awoke bent in agony. Moaning, I rolled onto my back, searching for relief. My husband, Tom, slept beside me, oblivious to my suffering. For a second, I resented him, but it passed when another sharp pain tore through my abdomen. I flopped around seeking release from the discomfort.

"Are you ok?" Tom grunted.

"No, I just wanted to wake up and moan a while," I sneered in the dark.

"Stomach pain? Again?"

"Yeah," I sighed. "I wish it would go away."

What is happening to me? Why does it happen every night? Will I ever get to sleep again?

Multiple specialists, an endoscopy, a colonoscopy, and a gallbladder function test showed nothing. The pain was real, but the medical tests failed to identify any cause.

Maybe it had more to do with my confidence taking a beating and the high level of stress under which I was trying to function. Each Monday I woke at 5:00 am, hurried to the airport, and flew to Philadelphia. Once I landed and got loaded into the rental car, I drove fifty miles to company headquarters. I stayed there several days, then returned home. Every. Single. Week. This commute was a new requirement. Before that, I worked remotely for seventeen years managing a small team of people and traveling to Pennsylvania only once every four to six weeks. With new management came new expectations, and the weekly commute commenced.

Alec and Vera came into the kitchen one Tuesday morning before school and asked, "Mom—why are you home? Aren't you supposed to be on a plane right now?" What a gut punch. I missed a lot of activities with our kids and felt guilty about it. The anxiety built up and weighed on me. My productivity suffered because either I was in meetings all day or traveling. The only time I got work done was in the hotel room at night, where I worked furiously to tackle mounting deadlines and commitments. I got it done working long hours and cutting sleep during the week. My work relationships, which I highly valued, started to be affected because I didn't have time for collaborative discussions anymore.

During this period, I reported to four different executive level managers in eighteen months. With each change in manager, my confidence wavered as I adapted to a new leadership style and adopted a new set of priorities. Each time, I justified my existence, my role, and my contribution, which made me question my value. With changes in expectations, the long weekly commute, and the shifting priorities, I started questioning the career that I spent thirty-three years building. *Was it worth it? What were my priorities? What will I be doing next week? Am I valued? Why do I constantly have to justify why I work here and what I contribute?*

Feeling undervalued and tense relationships with managers are two top reasons people leave jobs.

In 2014, there was another reorganization and another confidence blow. The C-suite carousel spun again, this time directly impacting our group. Corporate combined multiple teams within the company, each with a different set of customers, priorities, and incentives. Coalescing these disparate teams into one functioning organization was a tall feat that few leaders could successfully achieve. This reorganization did more than join the groups into one big unwieldy department. The entire organizational model was restructured around therapeutic areas instead of functional areas. Innovative Methods Development, the group I managed, no longer seemed valued. Attention to product teams was restricted, eliminating our team's access to critical information. Mechanisms to address questions closed. We were shut out. Instead of an open, collaborative environment, the new structure created silos. The pharmaceutical scientific research community is small, especially amongst epidemiologists, so we knew from our friends and colleagues that this organizational structure was far from optimal.

Unfortunately, strong female leaders were not embraced in this newly reorganized group. Questioning or engaging in intellectual debate about complex problems was discouraged. As a strong female leader, I enjoy debate about strategy, scientific methods, and study design within teams to drive the best decisions and possible outcomes. Each time I attempted to offer alternative options, it was evident that my ideas were not welcome, and my confidence took another hit. Disdain and tension escalated with each meeting I had with our new leader. I tried to adjust and prepare exactly what I thought was wanted, but I was always wrong. It did not matter what solution I brought to the table. If it came from me, it was not acceptable.

In one meeting early in this new leader's tenure, I was reviewing my workload and projects, one of which involved complex methodology. When queried about how that project would help the company, I responded, "It will help us understand how to design and analyze these types of common studies, in order to avoid bias." More details were requested. I described how we select variables to derive propensity scores based on their relationship to outcomes and exposure, and that the propensity score derived to control for confounding for one outcome or subgroup might not be appropriate for another. When I looked up, it was clear that what I was saying was not being understood. I asked, "Are you familiar with propensity scores?" Oops! It was out of my mouth before I could catch it.

Questioning the knowledge and capabilities of this new leader was not a good idea. The behavior expected by this leader was to conform and oblige without discussion. When the question popped out of my mouth, I saw her eyes blaze and her face turn red. I got stared down in stony silence. I waited. The moment stretched. Honestly, my intent was to help her understand the impact of these biases and methods on our studies. It was obviously an embarrassing situation. For whatever reason, she was unwilling to ask questions or appear unknowledgeable.

I broke the moment and launched into an explanation of propensity scores, digging my hole deeper.

After that awkward exchange, I knew my time was limited because I didn't want to work for a leader who was not willing or able to ask questions in order to understand the work being done. Epidemiology is complex; colleagues and leaders must engage in discussions to fully understand the work. It drew into sharper relief what I was already asking myself about staying or going.

Asking questions is a sign of confidence
and self-awareness.

The pain escalated. It not only visited me at night, but interrupted my daytime productivity and forced me to evaluate my physical and mental health. I realized that I couldn't live like this. The organization was no longer a good fit for me, my confidence was heading downhill, and my health was suffering. I needed to make a big change.

From the Beginning

To understand my confidence journey and relationship with anxiety, we need to visit my childhood. I've always loved the mountains of western North Carolina where I grew up but the things, I remember most about my childhood are independence and loneliness. I was the youngest of three children, with a sister five years older and a brother three years older. As kids, we left the house after homework on weekdays or cartoons on Saturday morning, went in different directions and came back at dusk. I wandered the neighborhood, playing basketball here, and horseshoes or badminton there. There were no close friends—our neighborhood didn't have any girls my age. I became one of the boys. We played basketball, pickleball, and baseball, but the boys didn't like a girl playing with them. My older brother sometimes stood up for me, but most of the time ignored me. I never really felt like I fit in or that I was good enough. I got lost reading books alone and practicing piano when the neighborhood boys wouldn't let me play ball.

My father worked in textiles and traveled to New York on the company jet every Monday morning, returning late Friday evening—a long weekly commute just like I wound up eventually doing in my own career. All that travel put stress on my dad as well as my mom, who was left raising three active kids alone. My siblings and I learned to be quiet and try to stay out of the way.

My parents were shocked to discover my sixteen-year-old brother was selling drugs at the high school and being sought by local police. Recognizing that my brother needed to get out of town, Dad took swift action. Ten years after moving into the neighborhood, we moved out of state, with only a few weeks to sell the house, pack, and relocate. Dad found a new job and moved our mom, my brother and me to Lake View, a small South Carolina (SC) community. My sister stayed in the Asheville area to attend technical college. This relocation had a substantial impact on me. I was thirteen years old, and my world turned upside down in a few short weeks. My friends, the size of my school, my home, the home environment— everything changed.

In this small town, everyone knew everyone, and everything about everyone. Random strangers asked, "Hey, are you the one that just moved into the old house by the Methodist church?" We were newcomers, and we did not fit in. I didn't even know how to fit in. I adjusted the way I spoke to adopt their southern drawl. We were there a year before we moved again, thirty minutes away, to a somewhat larger town called Dillon for a better school system.

My brother escaped trouble with the police by crossing state lines, but he refused to see a psychiatrist afterward, or at least be verbal with one. Just as my parents couldn't convince him to talk to a psychiatrist, they couldn't convince him to change schools for his senior year when we moved to Dillon. I didn't want to change schools and make new friends again either. We finally convinced our parents to let us stay at the same school, and my brother and I took a long bus ride every day. That year, an excellent teacher piqued my interest in math and boosted my confidence, giving me the mathematical foundation upon which I built my career in quantitative sciences. I obtained excellent grades in my first year of high school without trying too hard.

In Dillon, Mom got involved in the Welcome Wagon, which helped integrate her into the fabric of the community, and she introduced me to the lead volunteer's daughter, who was my age. This helped me form a close group of friends, I got involved in loads of activities, and my confidence grew. Mathematics was still my strongest subject, and high grades overall were easily achieved, freeing me up for fun with friends and school club activities.

However, Dad hated his job managing the mill in Lake View, and the summer before my senior year, we moved back to Asheville. I was devastated. This was the third move and school system in four years. I begged them not to move until I graduated high school or at least to let me stay with friends until I finished. No luck. They did not budge. I was angry and hurt.

I went months without speaking a word to anyone, including parents and teachers. I did not utter a word. I was invisible and silent at home. I was invisible and silent at Asheville High School. I avoided eye contact and made no friends. The classes were more challenging, and I had to study hard for the first time to get good grades for college admissions. The silence, the brooding anger, and the difficult schoolwork fueled my lack of confidence and depression. It was a dark time in my life, with what I now recognize as clinical depression without treatment. Low confidence and low self-esteem were familiar companions that led to fear and anxiety. My parents chalked all this up to a rebellious teen phase and thought little of it. There was no discussion, opening, or treatment options. I was expected to "just grow out of it."

I tried to escape my internal angst and tried anything to resolve my anger and depression. The summer before I went to college was wild. I smoked pot and drank with my summer work colleagues, hung out with a rough crowd that included unsavory characters, and worried my mom into her own anxiety. I was thrusting about in search of myself, my identity, and my confidence.

When college started, I moved into a dormitory, and was introduced to people that were smart, curious, friendly, and accepting of me as well as my insecurities. I ambitiously selected a dual major in mathematics and music as a freshman. Gradually, I spent less time with the rough crowd and more time with my new friends. I began to feel more like I belonged, but feelings of insecurity and being judged still lingered. My anxiety was tied to my lack of confidence and not feeling like I belonged, emotions which had been acute during the previous five years.

Other than my initial interest in math and music, no clear direction or career plan was apparent to me. I discovered my eventual career by happenstance. Someone walked into my third college calculus class with flyers announcing a new major called biostatistics, the application of statistics to biology and health problems. The calculus classes cranked up my anxiety and more advanced classes were required to secure a degree in math. I met with the professor coordinating the new biostatistics program, who was enthusiastic and energized my curiosity. In this field, I could use math to solve medical and biological problems. I could apply biostatistics to understand medical data, analyze it, and interpret results. This might be a way to build my confidence. I changed my major and was one of only eight students in the first full biostatistics undergraduate class at the University of North Carolina. With few undergraduate level classes yet available, we took masters level classes immediately. Although it was a highly demanding program, I was on solid ground and surrounded by people like me. My anxiety nibbled at the edges, but my confidence was growing.

My early years and academic journey were not all that smooth nor conducive to confidence building. Stress, anxiety, and low confidence seemed to be an underlying part of my life. The unexpected relocations after developing deep relationships, loneliness in the early years, drug use and rough crowds, and the constant sense of not belonging fueled my insecurities. The pressure was relentless to get good grades in college and not be like my brother who flunked out. This anxiety for perfection and high marks pursued me throughout my education. For many years, I had recurring nightmares about taking exams that I was not prepared for, or that somehow, I missed a class and never really graduated high school, thereby making me unqualified. This anxiety stemmed from a lack of confidence, and I carried it into my first career position.

I debated between two opportunities for my first job out of college. One was with the Department of Defense, using statistics to determine secret communication codes that might be used in wartime. The other was with a large pharmaceutical company, applying biostatistics to analyze clinical trial data. Both intrigued me, but the pharmaceutical company won, mainly due to recommendations of a respected advisor. I worked for this advisor for several semesters analyzing clinical trial data for pharmaceutical drug development and felt I was better prepared to take on this responsibility full time.

The pharmaceutical company that hired me was based in Philadelphia and required me to move. I forged out on my own to a new part of the country, a new city, and a big new job at twenty-one years old. My title was Associate Statistician in their phase 1 drug development area. I was the first to have that title because they had never hired someone with a bachelor's degree, only those with masters or doctorates. Phase 1 studies are the initial "first-in-man" studies to understand the pharmacokinetics of the drug and its safety in humans.

The first week, my manager gave me a large stack of hand-written and typed case-report forms. Case-report forms were how standardized data were collected in trials, before the advent of electronic data entry. He said, "Here's your first assignment," plopped down the massive pile of paper and walked away. I took the stack and arranged it on my desk. I read every form but was clueless as to what to do with the information. He came to my desk a week later and asked, "How's that study coming along?"

"What study?"

"You know that big stack of forms I gave you last week?" he cocked his head, curious.

"Oh yeah, here it is." I proudly showed him that it was in a prominent place on my desk.

He closed his eyes, pinched the bridge of his nose, and said, "Have you started to analyze it? It's due next week."

"OH.... You wanted me to analyze it?" I quipped. "But it's all paper forms!"

"You're supposed to enter the data first, then analyze it." He sighed, lifted his head, and looked at me.

A giggle burst out of my mouth. I replied, "I'm sorry, I wasn't sure what to do with it!"

"I guess maybe I should've been a little clearer about the expectations," he nodded and began to turn from my desk.

"Wait!" I nearly shouted. "I will enter that data now. What do we use to do that?" After losing a week, I was not going to go another second without asking the questions I needed to ask, in order to know how to do the job. And my manager admitted he needed to spend time training me. I was initially embarrassed, and it was a blow to my confidence, but I was young and just starting out. I did not know how things were done in this big organization. I learned early that I had to dive into being uncomfortable and ask questions. After our initial bump in the road, he and I worked well together, and he still is one of my favorite leaders. I settled in, worked furiously, took on new responsibilities, new jobs, and a host of other big assignments, all while hiding my anxiety and trying to build my confidence. I completed my masters and started my doctoral degree while working full time. Maybe I could educate myself out of anxiety and build my confidence.

After a particularly intense doctoral education week, I had my first panic attack when I got home from work one day. I was dating a man who lived in the apartment across the hall from me. I saw him with another woman. While we had not promised each other exclusivity, we were serious and tended to spend most of our free time together. I stood at my door with my eye to the peephole, waiting to spot him with her.

That night I watched them leave his apartment together. He put his hand on the small of her back after he shut his door. Then she slid her hand into his as they walked to the car. My breathing pitched. Hyperventilating, my heart pounded, my chest squeezed, and my pulse raced. Spots floated in my sight. I slid down hard onto my butt, shaking. The anxiety took over my physical body for the first time, but it would not be the last.

The next day I made an appointment with a psychoanalyst. I needed to take action to control the anxiety, and the panic attack scared me. Thankfully, the appointment was within a few days. Uncertainty tried to take over as I walked into her office. She attempted to put me at ease, but my nerves wouldn't let go. Through her gentle and patient questioning, I started to open up and explain why I was there. After two sessions with her, I thought things were going well. She sent me a letter stating that she could not be my therapist, because my situation was too close to her own, and she felt like she could not be objective. I put the letter down and asked myself if that was the definition of a bad day. *Did I just get rejected by my therapist?* She referred me to a new therapist who helped me identify and manage my triggers and anxiety. I still do some of the exercises she taught me.

When I start feeling anxious, I ask myself three questions:

- *Why am I feeling anxious? Is it this obvious situation or something more subtle?*
- *What is the worst possible outcome of this situation and who is impacted? Is that so bad?*
- *Do I need medical attention, or just to talk to a friend?*

The second question usually grounds me. I recognize that there are many worse outcomes, and life goes on. She suggested that my lack of confidence could partially stem from the stress as a child with my father constantly traveling and my mother trying to keep it together while solely raising three kids. Therapy was hugely helpful and illuminating and provided tools to help me through difficult times.

Although the panic attack was triggered by a personal situation, I applied the coping skills I learned to my work environment. I finished my doctoral degree, did fellowships, and traveled the world on business, all while keeping anxiety down and attempting to build my confidence with each milestone. I loved my job. The career I chose was a great fit for me. I worked at an incredible company that firmly believed in science and I was surrounded by respected mentors. I was a hard, reliable worker and pushed myself to gain my colleagues' respect.

The underlying anxiety drove me to deliver results above and beyond my male colleagues, or really, any other colleague. This resulted in long hours and extensive preparatory work before meetings and presentations. Because of my low confidence, performance review time made me apprehensive, even though my bosses and colleagues praised me, my leadership, and my work. I hid the underlying low self-esteem, but Imposter Syndrome eroded my confidence and followed me throughout my career. My sister and I used to joke about people finding us out, uncovering that we weren't as good as people thought we were. Perhaps this was further validation that the lack of confidence and not feeling accepted may have stemmed from our childhood. My father's mantra was: "No one is indispensable. Anyone, no matter how good, can be replaced."

I led successful large initiatives for the company, led multiple academic methodological research projects, served on executive level document review committees for protocols across therapeutic areas and the corporation, supported interactions with regulatory agencies, and was recognized as a leader in my field in the industry. I approached work with a positive attitude every day, and people perceived me as confident and capable. All of this should have built my confidence. Outwardly, I showed confidence and spoke up. Inwardly, I was insecure, but I hid it well.

I hated speaking in public. My career included delivering presentations at professional society meetings, and I recognized it was an essential part of the job. I was on the edge of a panic attack, with clammy, shaky hands and dry mouth each time I gave a big presentation. They say the more you speak in public, the easier it becomes. That wasn't true for me, at least not until the pressures of the corporate world were in the rearview mirror.

In 2012, I was promoted to co-leading a group that focused on methodological aspects of the post-marketing needs for product safety and for reimbursement, to ensure these aspects were considered throughout a development program. It was a high-profile job that needed deep methodological expertise and strong leadership. I was hesitant to take it, but the job was perfect for me. Then multiple reorganizations occurred, new executives rolled in, and the weekly travel started and literally made me sick. My dad traveled the entire week for most of my childhood, and that had a huge impact on me. *Was I willing to do something like Alec and Vera? To myself?*

From Anxiety to Confidence

In late 2014, as part of the final reorganization, senior leadership offered me a job that would require relocating to Philadelphia. I was already beating myself up for not being home like my dad, and now they wanted me to move my kids during their final high school years. I would not put my children into my own awful experience of changing schools late in high school. I declined the position and retired from the company. With my retirement, the nighttime and daytime inexplicable stomach pains stopped, and I slept better. I felt better. I was better.

It was freeing. For the first time in my adult life, I did not have a corporate committee or senior management asking me to justify my value and my projects at every turn. I did not know exactly what I wanted to do next, but I knew I would not join a large corporation. I was done with that. I thought I might try consulting. I'd always been curious about it, and it seemed like the ideal life with lots of flexibility, and the ability to choose your projects and select whom you worked with. *But could I do it? Would I be successful? How would I get clients? Would I have any clients?*

Looking back, it was only my anxious mind and lack of confidence asking those questions. I fretted and fretted, until Tom said, "Honey, it doesn't matter. Do it because you want to, not because you have to." This released me from the high expectations that are paramount in an over-achiever. "Don't worry, just try it and see."

It made me feel better because I knew I had support. I was still uncertain because I was used to clear goals to drive my direction. But I tried to relax. I reminded myself that I didn't have nearly the levels of stress and anxiety that I did when working in corporate America. No reorganizations. No new managers with different priorities. I was my own boss. I set my own course and business strategy. I chose whether to take on new projects and with whom to work. It was a fresh perspective and a relief to my stress.

I created a LinkedIn profile indicating myself as a consultant and launched a website that showed my portfolio of services. I was hired within weeks by a previous colleague. One thing led to another, and I had four clients within three months and worked twenty consistent hours a week, exactly aligning with my goals. I was collaborating on methodology and strategy, running, and building a company, and developing different types of relationships. The new work built my confidence and because clients hired me for my expertise, I felt valued. They listened to what I had to recommend. I did not have to constantly prove my worth.

The firm grew organically. Colleagues were interested in collaborating with me on projects, and previous colleagues were interested in leaving big pharmaceutical companies. Before I knew it, I was running a multi-million-dollar pharmacoepidemiology consulting firm, managing over thirty consultants, and working with over fifty pharmaceutical firms, providing services on strategy and methods for observational studies, real-world evidence and patient reported outcomes. I spent four years on the Board of Directors for my field's professional society and was nominated as a fellow. I even co-edited a textbook.

Now in my early sixties, through all the consulting projects we provide, and with running my company, I finally have the confidence I always felt I needed. I recognize the value that our experienced consultants bring, and I know that we provide good advice and rigorous, high-quality products. Finally, I recognize that I don't have to have all the answers on hand. No one is perfect. I learned to say, "I don't know, but I can certainly research it if you'd like." And I do.

Accept who you are. No one is perfect. No one should be expected to have all the answers.

Mental health is a subject that is not discussed in the workplace but should be. Anxiety and depression are almost taboo topics; yet these conditions can have a major impact on employee productivity and collaboration with others. People with anxiety or depression might feel less alone dealing with issues if their manager were aware. However, it should not be a mandate to disclose such conditions due to privacy. Sharing must be at the employee's discretion. It is certainly plausible that resources and courses on coping mechanisms could be provided while still protecting the privacy of individual employees' mental health conditions.

My low confidence and my sense of not belonging were sources of stress and anxiety over many years. I carried this with me from my childhood, through my academic experience, and into my career, and these feelings drove my perfectionist or overachiever attributes. Not feeling accepted for who I was or for what I contributed stemmed not from my professors, mentors, or managers, but from my own inner voice, and my own fears and insecurities. It was self-inflicted. I finally chose to love and accept myself, and this built my confidence. Hopefully you will embrace your authentic inner self much earlier in your life and career than I did. Be brave, be bold, and unleash your confidence onto the world.

INTRODUCING DR. AMANDA JAMES

Dr. Amanda James is a leader in higher education, adjunct faculty member, and advocate for individuals to achieve self-realization. Her career spans multiple industries, coast to coast, with extensive expertise in managing recruitment and enrollment. Amanda's personal and professional focus is to help others achieve their goals and build meaningful, successful lives. As a leader, Amanda creates a safe and inclusive workplace that builds strong, lasting relationships with team members and creates collaborative, integrated teams. She strives to help her employees and colleagues identify and follow their own passions and pushes them to realize that loving the work, finding hobbies that bring fulfillment, and having experiences that promote personal growth are what life is all about. Her drive to help students succeed is evident in the work she does through every step of their educational journey both inside and outside of the classroom. Amanda lives in South Carolina with her husband, two beautiful and lively children, and sweet Basset Hound. Amanda enjoys traveling, reading, hosting events for her coworkers, and watching British baking shows.

I'VE GOT THIS!

Through four different industries, three graduate degrees, mistakes, and successes, I challenged and pushed myself to do more, and to do better. In these experiences I developed an *I've got this* mindset. I faltered and doubted myself but with each success, each lesson learned, each opportunity for me to overcome, my confidence and self-assuredness grew.

Before 2020, I thought I had overcome all my biggest challenges and life couldn't throw any new curve balls at me, but I was wrong. In January, an experience changed my life forever, and it made me question everything I knew. I realized my prior experiences had not prepared me for this event. It was a moment of celebration and excitement, which I still carry with me, as I try to navigate my new normal. I push forward into this chaotic and unpredictable life.

Conversations about attending college started before junior high school. My parents set the expectation of hard work and a four-year completion; if I took any longer to graduate, I would have to pay for my college education. College was a routine dinner table discussion. My parents and I talked about different options, and there were no limits on which university they encouraged me to consider. And still, when it was time to decide where to go for my bachelor's degree, it was a difficult process and a difficult choice. I was accepted into excellent schools, but my parents were concerned about my success on a large campus. I did not want to hear their opinions, because at seventeen I knew everything! I reluctantly agreed to a final visit to a small private college. Within thirty minutes on campus, I knew it was the place for me. I was enamored with the people, the programs, and the campus experience. My parents were right; I needed extra support, hand holding, and the check-ins from professors. I only had four years to graduate. I couldn't waste time getting lost or going through multiple phases of finding myself.

It was the absolute right decision for me. I met incredible professors, made good friends, and worked hard. My most trusted professors encouraged me to continue my education after graduation. And I did just that. The MBA program was a hybrid program which allowed me to study online and work full-time outside of school. It was a lot of work, but the design worked well for me and helped me focus on my priorities as I entered the real world. I lived by my calendar and reminded myself regularly that *I've got this.*

I had no clear career plan after earning my bachelor's degree. I would find a job when I figured out where I wanted to live and just go from there. With my mom's help, I landed my first job as a teacher's assistant in a high school class of students who had behavioral and emotional problems. The course I taught was Life Skills. At twenty-two years old, with limited life experience, I worked with these students to teach them how to look for a job, rent an apartment, and make healthy food choices. I was young, fresh out of college, and I had a job that required me to help and guide high school students. The students did not receive grades in the class I taught, and some would miss school for weeks at a time because they were in juvenile hall. They spent nights and weekends working or taking care of family members while their parents were unavailable. School wasn't their top priority.

During one of the lessons about making healthy food choices, the lead teacher and I had the idea to start a class garden. The idea was to teach the students that growing their own food was possible and not challenging. What could possibly be wrong with this plan? Well, things got out of hand quickly as they talked about the money they could make selling marijuana grown using the class garden. *Wait, what?* These high school kids knew more about running a business or a side hustle than I did. The idea of growing pot wasn't what caught me off guard; it was how open and brazen they were talking about it. At school. In front of their teachers.

The garden lesson was just one of a few experiences in this job that decreased my confidence because with each day, I realized that I was unable to relate to them. I couldn't understand their world and that absence of a connection led to a lack of confidence—*I absolutely don't got this.* The fact that my personal life was so different from these students' lives and their world, their experiences, made me realize how fortunate and sheltered I was. This job and these students shaped me and my decisions about my future career. I knew that I wanted to make a positive impact and a difference in the lives of students.

After three weeks, I knew teaching high school was not going to be my long-term career. I stayed the entire year to learn as much as I could from the job and the students. At the end of the year, my professional confidence was developing as the students, when talking with me about their plans for their future, showed signs of understanding the skills I had taught them. One personal goal took shape: I knew I wanted to work in a field that helped others. At this point, I was nine months into my MBA program and was managing the schoolwork while teaching, but I was not confident that I could continue to be successful if I made a career change.

When the school year ended, I went back to my college town to spend more time with my friends and search for a new job. I only knew I wanted to help people—like really helping them. I kept thinking, *I've got this,* as I applied to job after job that fell into the big bucket of helping people. I applied to non-profits, hospitals, community centers, even schools; and even though I believed *I've got this,* I was not landing any interviews. Mom threw me another lifeline and introduced me to an accounting firm that was hiring. I thought *Accounting, really? How was I going to make a lasting and impactful change in people's lives doing accounting?*

Accounting was not the plan I had in mind or the vision for my next job, but it was my only option and data entry was easy enough. I also took this as a sign to stay focused on my studies. I had completed one year of a three-year master's program when I started at the accounting firm. With this job, I made finishing my MBA my top priority. Shifting my priorities was not an easy decision to make because, as practical as it was to have accounting experience, the transformative experience at the high school moved me, and now I was just crunching numbers. I enjoyed my colleagues and clients, but my confidence took a hit in this role. *Do I have this?*

A new client joined the firm after realizing he was unable to continue to do the books for his personal business. The first step for our company was to perform an audit of his books. This meant looking at his income and expenses, bank and credit card statements, and a pile of work that had not been reconciled for nearly a year. While the task was daunting, I was part of the team selected to do it. So, I rolled up my sleeves and dug in—*I've got this.* This was the beginning of the end of my confidence in this job.

To complete the work for the audit, I had to process and calculate everything by hand. With each reconciliation that I was off $2. 30 or $. 54 cents or $1. 17, my confidence went with it. Each time it did not match up perfectly, I had to start from the beginning until the ticker tape on the 10-key machine matched the statement. I spent hours upon hours on this work and with each mistake I realized—I *don't got this.* I did eventually get it all done through brute force and persistence, but I did not feel strong or confident about it.

While the work brought challenges, the lack of interaction with people is what left me struggling the most. I am an extrovert and needed more social interaction with others, and I missed the unexpected daily challenges at the high school. The job supported my lifestyle, I made friends in the office, and it allowed me to continue my studies. I stayed longer than expected, but looking back, I am glad that I did not get stuck there. Many people stay in an unsatisfying job because it is good enough but unfulfilling. After two years at the company, and finally finishing my MBA program, I got an unexpected push to make a change—from a client.

One night, a tax client, named Mary, came in. As I was working through her documents, she asked me questions about myself, my job and if I liked it. I answered them almost honestly, I mean I was at work, and she was going to meet with my boss. My responses were short and polite. After she left my office, my boss popped her head in and asked about our conversation. I panicked. I did not want to get fired for saying this job wasn't my long-term plan. I didn't have to worry though because what my boss said next was surprising. She told me that Mary was a psychic and read auras. If I was open to it,

Mary wanted to share what she saw in me. Completely caught off-guard, I responded with "I would love to talk with her more." I was willing to do almost anything to help point me in a clear direction, and I knew accounting was not my final career. I had never had my aura read nor even met a psychic before, but I figured what could it hurt? *I've got this!*

A few days later Mary called, and our session began. She told me that she could see I was not destined to work in accounting and that my calling is working with people, and specifically to help people better their lives. This woman did not know me, had only spent fifteen minutes with me, and she knew that I was in the wrong job. It was a sign. It was confirmation and it was the push I needed to make a career change. I had to take a leap of faith into what I was supposed to be doing with my life. I had to be confident and believe that—*I've got this*. Aside from work, she told me that I would meet a wonderful man to share my life with and that I would write a book someday.

Tax season ended in April and by May, I leapt! I quit the accounting role and gave myself time to find a job where I was helping people. Without a job lined up, or even a plan, for that matter, I told myself—*I've got this*. With the jolt from Mary, a new MBA, and work experience, I was confident I would find something that better aligned with my dreams. While I was ready to take on the world, I knew I needed a fallback plan. Accounting would be my fallback plan but without a degree in accounting, landing a job in that field would be hard. So, I found a fifteen-month Master of Accounting program and started in August.

After leaving the accounting firm, I was advised to use a recruiter to help me find a new job, one that would align with my goals and aspirations. This was the first time I heard about the recruiting profession. Three short months after leaving the accounting firm and a few days after starting another master's program, I landed a role as a recruiter which allowed me to help accounting and finance professionals find jobs. This one suggestion set in motion a fulfilling and enjoyable career.

My personality, accounting experience, and passion for helping others were the reasons I was hired into this new role. The job was different from anything I had done before—it was sales. I cold-called companies with open positions and assured them I would find their ideal candidates. I posted ads online and met with candidates to determine if they were the right fit for open roles I had in my purview. Throughout the training, I told myself *I've got this.*

A few weeks into the role I got my first job order for a client who needed a staff accountant that could start within two weeks. I was so excited that I completely blanked on asking the clarifying questions: pay, years of experience, software knowledge—you know, the basics about any job. Instead, I quickly replied, "Of course! I will send resumes over before the end of the day." And I hung up. My teammates cheered on my first job order and then reminded me that I had no information about the actual position or what the client was looking for. News about my excitement, and blunder, spread across the office with congratulatory comments and stories of coworkers doing the same thing.

After this initial blunder, my confidence increased with every role filled, every happy candidate, every satisfied hiring manager, and every paycheck that was higher than the one before. It was a perfect fit for me. I was twenty-five years old, living with girlfriends, fulfilling my passion for helping others, getting paid, and I was good at my job. Not every job or candidate was perfect, but with more experience, the better and better I got at making lasting matches. *I've got this.*

My recruiting career started at a large company and after gaining experience and knowing myself and my capabilities better, I thought it might be time for a change.

Luckily, I knew how to find a job. *I've got this.* I wanted to work in a smaller firm that expanded the types of roles I was assigned beyond accounting and finance. *I've got this.* I took more than fifteen months to complete my second master's degree because work got busy, and the need for the degree felt less important with my work and financial success.

With two years of recruiting work experience and a new master's in accounting, I left the large company and joined a boutique firm where I continued to grow my career in recruiting. My paychecks grew and I had some of the best bosses in my career. I developed relationships with hiring managers who trusted me to fill jobs across all fields—marketing, technology, sales, administrative. I was taught to develop relationships with companies, not just individuals. I was supported personally. I was challenged to exceed an ever-higher set of goals. I told myself—*I've got this.*

During this time at the boutique firm, I realized that I wanted more from my life. I did not yet know what that was exactly, but I started to get restless at work. While every day was different—new clients, new jobs, excited job applicants—the excitement and motivation started to dwindle. The paychecks would reignite my passion but with each passing month, the motivation disappeared faster. I knew I needed a shake-up; I just didn't know what. Along comes my mother, again, with a story about her coworker whose daughter started a doctoral program that allowed her to continue working full-time. It took about three seconds for me to be intrigued and start my own research for doctoral programs. I mean, I managed to earn two masters while working, I can do a doctorate too—right? *I've got this.* So, without a real plan as to how I was going to use this doctorate, I stayed in my job, started the program, and got back into the groove of working full-time and being in school full-time. *I've got this.*

It was settled, I continued my work as a recruiter and on the evenings and weekends when I was not working, I was completing coursework, spending time with my family and friends, and trying to have a social life. As with life, and as Mary predicted, I met a wonderful man, Andrew, whom I fell in love with and married, much to my mother's relief. Throughout the relationship, conversations about our future made me reflect on my career choices and what my future as a recruiter looked like. While the job was amazing, it was also non-stop. I was available all the time—nights and weekends which worked for me as a single woman. But would this work in my new marriage?

On our honeymoon the emails and phone calls poured

in, and we both realized the magnitude of my commitment to this career. My husband is understanding and patient but the realization that even on vacation, my honeymoon, I would be working was jarring to both of us. It was the sign I needed that it was time to reevaluate my priorities. I was almost two years into my doctoral program, still not entirely sure how to use it, but I had a clear desire to find a career that provided me the ability to follow my calling of helping people and have a healthy work-life balance. I decided it was time to make a career change and leave recruiting.

The idea of working in higher education was sparked during my undergrad years. There were a host of professors who were inspirational, kind, energetic, smart women who raved about the work they did helping students earn a degree and were leaders in their respective fields. These conversations came flooding back to me and helped focus my decision on how I was going to use my doctorate degree. In my five years of recruiting, the amazing network I developed led to my career in higher education. I thought it was the perfect career choice that fulfilled my desire to help people. Plus, I had such a wonderful experience with each of the institutions I attended that it was an obvious place to start.

What I was not prepared for was the massive cut in

pay and different means to measure and quantify my success. I was accustomed to a certain lifestyle and level of confidence that was based on exceeding goals and being paid accordingly—this got chucked out the window when I entered higher education. With my background in recruitment, I simply convinced a private institution to have me help build a career development center for their college of extended learning. My fiercest advocate and supporter, Andrew, convinced me it was OK to take the pay cut and to follow this dream into higher education. With his support, it was time to test these waters and decide if this was my final career destination. After accepting the job, I realized how different this assignment was from my previous positions. I reminded myself— *I've got this.*

The college was growing, and I was hard at work creating a career development center. With the rapid growth of the school, new positions were created, and one aligned with my background perfectly. I was promoted to leading the admissions team and managing the partnerships with the local two-year institutions.

The programs offered by the college of extended learning were geared toward adult learners. The students in these programs wanted to earn their bachelor's degree but couldn't attend classes on the main campus, so the courses were offered hybrid with in-person sessions being held at the two-year institutions around the county. I completed my graduate level education with hybrid learning and brought that experience into the program. Working with non-traditional students was challenging because they had to make sure the timing and financial investment worked with their family schedules and needs. These students knew the degree would help them advance in their careers or, for some, put them on a new career path.

Everything was new, the team, the infrastructure, and at times it felt like we were building the plane as we were flying it. We created an entirely new educational model that did not yet exist in California. While the newness was exciting, I was in an unknown role, in an industry where I had no previous work experience, and working with a new team that was trying to establish processes to support the students who were already enrolled. This led to quite a few mistakes and quite a few moments of questioning my decision. *Do I got this?* I couldn't push my admissions counselors like I did my recruiters; there was no financial incentive. I couldn't expect people to work around the clock like we did in recruiting; it wasn't the culture. There were many moments when I questioned both my ability to do the job and be an effective leader. A few—*I don't got this*—moments during my first year had me questioning whether higher education was the right career choice for me.

I have been lucky to have extraordinary women in my life, and I had a tremendous boss and amazing coworkers who helped me learn the landscape, understand the processes, and work through questions and issues as they arose. However, the paychecks did not validate my efforts and did little to fuel my confidence. I had to find this validation and confidence in other areas.

During the first year in this role, my confidence came from improving and developing processes, hiring and training new admissions counselors, seeing the enrollment numbers increase, and being part of a program that helped people better their lives. This too became evident when I was offered the opportunity to teach a class for the RN to BSN program. With two master's degrees and nearly finished with my doctoral program, I met the qualifications to teach. My first course was titled "Cultural Influences in the Workplace" and was directly applicable to the nursing profession. The classroom interactions, while different from my first teaching job, brought back those same feelings of excitement as I watched the students understand the course content and listened to stories about applying what they had learned in their daily work-lives. My passion for being in the classroom and working with students was invigorating and my confidence grew as I connected with each student. I was on the right path and then life threw us in a new direction.

Andrew had an incredible job opportunity, but it was on the other side of the country and required us to relocate. We were the perfect targets for this new role, partially because we did not have kids. When we made the decision to move, I comforted myself by accepting that although the work with these students was over, I would use my passion and confidence and continue at another institution. *I've got this.*

No two companies or institutions of higher education are the same. The programs offered might be the same, but the culture, community and experience are unique to each campus. I was looking for a purple squirrel, a university that was both academically rigorous to help students achieve greatness while also being supportive and inclusive to all. I spent months looking at institutions within an hour's drive of our new home. When I finally met the staff, students, and faculty at my current job it was an easy decision to join the new institution and community. With my experience in higher education, coupled with my passion to help all students, I thought I was ready to hit the ground running. *I've got this!*

In this new role, I had to determine how to keep my confidence validated—exceeding the enrollment goals was an indicator but leaving my confidence in the hands of young people's decisions did not seem wise. The work, the daily interactions with my team members, the excitement on the students' faces when they stepped on campus, and the conversation with parents are what validated my performance and my confidence. I get up every day and know that I am the best one for this job and why this is my ultimate career.

With the career change, cross-country move and a few other life events, my doctoral program took a few more years than I had anticipated but I did it. *I've got this!* As I am living my most confident life at work as Dr. Amanda James, gaining new knowledge, making mistakes, and working to build an environment that people love working in, January 2020 came and—BOOM!—my life changed forever.

A year prior, my husband and I decided to embark on a new journey, which pushed me to compartmentalize confidence into buckets of work confidence and home confidence. In January 2020, we welcomed our son, Anderson, to our family. I was not worried. Kids are the next phase in life. The first year was beautiful, unique, and challenging. I told myself *I've got this whole parenting thing.* Yep. One year in and I was a seasoned pro.

When Anderson started walking and learned the word no, I realized I had no idea what I was doing. Work life seemed so much more straightforward, even in higher education where the numbers and paychecks weren't always the indicators of success. At work you can research, study, learn, and apply those learnings to your job; at home this whole other being had his own mind, decisions, influence, and control. Each of Anderson's milestones came with a slew of opportunities to learn how to be a good mom. I researched and read everything I could get my hands on. I felt comfortable saying I am a good mom, not a great mom or perfect mom because there is no such thing. Most moms, most parents, are making things up as they go, and I continually remind myself—*I've got this.*

Making things up as I go works in most cases, but each day brings a new challenge. For example, one day he loves broccoli, the next day he won't touch it. While I try to guess what Anderson will eat, I need to know what he is learning in school. I have become a multi-linguist deciphering what he is saying when he learns a new word— this is much easier when I know what he did, learned or watched that day. I must be aware of what I say and how I say it because he repeats everything. Everything.

One sunny day we were driving home from daycare, and someone cut me off. I slammed on the brakes, and I yelled the f-word! I froze, gripping the wheel, and hoped he didn't hear it. Anderson, my sweet boy, with the sweetest voice, proceeded to repeat it over and over, and raised his voice with each announcement of the offending word. He repeated it enough to drown out my requests for him to stop. The thought of being embarrassed in front of other daycare parents when Anderson chants the f-word washed over me. Oh boy—*I definitely do not got this.* No schooling, work experience or reading mommy blogs helped me develop any confidence about my mom skills.

And even though some comfort comes from my friends with children, I don't know if it really makes me feel better or if I am just sharing my distress. Almost two years after my son's arrival, we had a daughter, Alice. Throughout my pregnancy and her first few months of life, I kept telling myself, we are working through all of this with our son, so when my daughter hits this age, we will be prepared. I shared this thought with someone at work who laughed in my face and said, "My two kids could not be any different. Good luck!" Well, at least I am prepared to do it trial-and-error style. Knowing that there is not a right way, no one way, or no book that I can read to know how to be a good parent; if my children are healthy, kind, and try their best, I will give myself grace and concede that I am a pretty good mom. At the end of the day, whatever my children try to throw at me—literally and figuratively—I know, *I've got this.*

My confidence, and the validation of my confidence, has shifted over the years with different experiences and different measures. Earning multiple degrees helped build my confidence as a young lady. These were trophies earned—real documents that proved my effort and ability. Each step of my career built on itself, shaped my dreams, and with the changes in my career, the measures of success changed.

As a young teacher with disadvantaged students, I found my passion in helping people. My confidence was built with the success and growth of the students. The experience in accounting served as a foundation and backstop for building for my future. It served as a steppingstone to my career in recruiting, where I recruited financial and accounting professionals. The candidate placement numbers, and big paychecks validated my *I've got this* mantra. Then moving into higher education, confidence was gained through developing my team, my organization, and the students' success rates. As a mom, as a career woman, as a human being, I am still learning and growing in my confidence.

The mantra *I've got this* has served me well and allowed me to enter new experiences and new challenges with a sense of excitement and hope. It focused me on what can be done and how, even if there are setbacks and mistakes, I will lean forward because *I've got this.*

As Mary predicted, I have written a book, well, a chapter of a book. She saw something in me, she asked permission to share, and her courage changed the trajectory of my life. I share my story to let you know that—*You've got this.* Even when you think you don't, even when your toddler is yelling the f-word at daycare, you've got this. Use a mantra, share a story, support the women and people in your life, and your confidence will grow with each mistake and each challenge overcome.

Even with the degrees, the career changes, and the realignment of how my confidence is fueled, sometimes it helps knowing that someone is, or has been, in your shoes. I confidently walk into my office each day knowing that my work will make a lasting impact on someone's life and eight hours later I walk into my house uncertain and rarely prepared to handle what my toddler and infant have waiting for me. But it's OK, because—*I've got this.*

INTRODUCING JENNIFER PESTIKAS

Jen Pestikas has always been a type-A super achiever. She was the straight A's student who was devastated when she got a B. Jen held herself to the highest standards and needed to check all the boxes that defined a successful life. After she grew up, that super achieving nature followed her to her career into the corporate world.

After twenty years in corporate, climbing the ladder in financial services from a bank teller to a Senior Vice President and doing "all the right things," Jen's health plummeted when she burned out. After years of striving, she was empty and broken—without energy and direction in her career and life.

While the time of healing that followed was hard, it was also a gift. It made Jen realize she didn't need to be perfect. She could give herself a measure of grace, she did not need to check all the successful life boxes, and she did not have to be superwoman. Jen understood what she wanted for the first time in her life. She wanted was to give back to women to help them avoid the same traps of striving, perfectionism, and not living their truth.

Jen is the founder and CEO of Brave Women at Work; a platform of services designed to amplify and develop female leaders. She is a certified career and leadership coach, the author of *Brave Women at Work: Stories of Resilience,* and the host of the Brave Women at Work podcast. If you would like to learn more about Jen and how she helps women, please visit her website at www. bravewomenatwork. com or connect with her via LinkedIn.

IMPOSTER

"I don't want to speak at your funeral," I declared, staring at RJ with a frown.

"Ah, Jen," He slurred. "I don't want you to either."

Other than the first-class flight attendant keeping his glass full, the flight was uneventful. RJ was my boss, my friend, and my mentor. I was his right-hand man. He praised me constantly and he was an excellent confidence builder. We grew close over the five years we worked together. RJ liked to party, like Mick Jagger, which was fitting because he was an avid Rolling Stones fan.

RJ brushed off my comment and said I shouldn't worry. He had everything under control. The moment passed with my intuition burning a hole in my psyche. *How could he make it like this another year?* I never experimented with his drugs of choice, so maybe I was just paranoid or scared. *Maybe it is all fine.* Maybe his work-hard, play-hard philosophy was normal, and I was just a square. We were leaving Las Vegas after all, where he could imbibe in his vices. He stayed out all night, doing God knows what, then shuffled in the next day disheveled and awry. He plodded through the day and began to perk up only when it seemed acceptable to start drinking again.

RJ was an *old* forty-seven-year-old and while he appeared to be in decent shape, he wasn't. On one hand, he always attracted attention from females with his good looks and charm, on the other hand his body was failing. He had crippling back pain that forced him to shuffle around the office. And his drinking didn't help. Over our five years together, I had seen more than one hangover, but as he half-slept on the flight home he looked different. Haggard, laconic, and sluggish. His countenance and physique were crying for rest. I was concerned.

When we got back to work, my worry took a back seat as things slid into our normal manic pace. RJ was the Vice President of Wealth Management for our team of ten. RJ and I worked together each day, and for the most part, I didn't notice any decline. He was supportive, always boosting me up and telling me what an incredible leader I was and would become. Workdays were often a blur of meetings, projects, and discussions. The organization followed the work-hard-play-hard philosophy commingling work and partying together. It drove the team to consistently deliver above and beyond expectations. We worked long hours, nights, weekends, and holidays. Celebrating with the team was a way to relax and thank them for the intensity we demanded. Maybe it was dysfunctional and not sustainable, but it was effective. That team outperformed any team I have seen in my career.

A few months later, RJ invited the group to a meeting at our favorite watering hole. This was not uncommon and maybe I should have noticed how often we drank together, but we all went to the pub for drinks and discussion. One drink turned into many more. After the twang of intuition on the flight, I started to observe RJ more closely. He drank Grey Goose vodka martinis with blue cheese stuffed olives. He swirled and twirled his glass, the ice clinked, the viscous liquid turned into a snow globe. He drank one after the other, and I wondered how he was standing. And then, out of nowhere, he questioned the table, "Do any of you have any pain medication?"

We had an altercation that night when I was leaving. I was the first one to leave. He grabbed my arm and asked me where I was going. Somehow, I felt I was doing something wrong, like leaving work earlier than anyone else, but we were at a bar. The bar was loud, and no one noticed. He hissed obscenities at me and cut me down with a painful personal attack. I was taken aback, pulled my arm loose, and then cried the way home in my car.

With more clarity the next day, I told John, my husband, what happened. We agreed I would quit the following week. I stayed. I did not quit, and I don't know why. Maybe it was comfort. Maybe it was because our team was intertwined personally and professionally. I knew I needed to leave, but I didn't have the courage or confidence. Fate would part us soon anyway.

After the incident in the bar, RJ and I were barely speaking. All in a rush, RJ decided to get back surgery. On a Friday, before the whole team was to attend another conference, he stopped by my office. His face was pasty and the dark circles that bruised his eyes belied his poor health. He was not well; I saw it. He was a shadow of the man he was a few months before, and even though I was still hurt and angry, those feelings dissipated when I saw him. He had aged ten years in two weeks. "Aren't you going to give me a hug and wish me well?" he needled me. I gave him a hug and wished him luck with the surgery.

The next Monday, my teammates and I trekked through Chicago O'Hare Airport on our way to the conference in Atlanta. The team was excited to go away for a few days to network with colleagues and to enjoy warmer weather.

RJ was a legend in our industry, and everyone wanted to know where he was. "Where's that rascal RJ?" "Where's our buddy, RJ?" As we tittered over drinks, we decided we would call him and tell him all the fun he was missing.

The phone rang and went to voicemail. I called again and again and heard his jovial voice telling me to leave a message. Everyone else at the bar seemed unbothered but my stomach dropped, and I sobered up. I stepped away from the noise into a narrow hall outside of the bathroom and called again. The phone was answered.

"RJ?" I whispered into the receiver.

"Jen, it's me. It's Ron."

"Why are you answering RJ's phone?"

"RJ passed."

Ron, one of my co-workers and RJ's closest friends, uttered impossible words. He continued to speak, but I could not hear what he was saying. His words were garbled and fading. I slid down the wall, wailing. I was lost. The phone clattered to the floor and spun in a slow circle.

"Jen?" the receiver announced. "Jen. Are you there?"

Was I here? Where was I?

Ron's persistence broke through the fog, and I reached for my phone. Sniffling and wiping away the fresh tears, I mewled, "Yes. I am here."

"You need to tell the team and get them home," Ron stated. "Can you do that?"

The next week was a blur. Telling the team, coordinating the emergency return, conversations with RJ's wife, and navigating our actual work, was done while I was numb and blind. I went through the motions in a haze of sadness. RJ's wife asked me to do the eulogy. Yes, of course I would. That is what I do. I say yes. I do all the things. That is what I do.

I delivered the eulogy, and everyone marveled at how I got through it. I don't remember a word. The only thing that played in an endless loop in my tenacious brain was the words I uttered on the flight home from Vegas. "I don't want to speak at your funeral."

The fallout of RJ's passing made the office feel like a wake. The team was suffering, and each person dealt with their grief in their own way. We lost our leader and friend, and it left a gaping hole that no one could possibly fill. I didn't realize I was so dependent on RJ for his praise and approval; he was my external source of confidence. Now that he was gone, I pushed my grief aside and focused on self-doubt, over-analyzing, and overworking. I thought I could work myself out of the grief. I thought when the going gets tough, the tough get going. And that's exactly what I did.

Within weeks, there was talk about shutting down our department temporarily or indefinitely. It was rumored that the CEO was unsure of what to do next. How could he possibly replace a legend like RJ? When I heard the rumor, a jolt of energy raced through me. I knew what to do. Completely out of character, I marched up to the CEO's office and scheduled his next available meeting time.

During our discussion, I asked him to make me the interim lead of the department in lieu of shutting down the organization. I was terrified of what I was saying, but I didn't want to let our team go. Little did I know that I was signing up for an eighteen-month crash course in confidence and Imposter Syndrome.

It happened. I was named Interim Manager of our organization, which had previously been run by the greatest of all time. I naïvely and proudly accepted the opportunity. After my acceptance, I stupidly thought it would come with a title change and pay increase. Lesson number one, negotiate title and pay before accepting interim positions. The CEO visited our department a few times to see how the team was doing after the announcement. He must have felt comfortable because we were largely left alone after those initial few visits. It felt like our team was floating apart, disconnected from the broader organization, drifting in our collective sadness. I had to lead them through it.

As the days and weeks wore on, I welcomed an enormous wave of Imposter Syndrome. Imposter Syndrome, the feeling of being a fraud, washed over me every time I spoke with a team member, or led a meeting. The team said things like, "Well, RJ used to do it this way" or "Did RJ teach you how to do this?" The nasty voice inside my head asked me questions like, *Who do you think you are, trying to replace RJ?* and *When do you think they are going to replace you because you're not good enough for this role?* My anxiety cranked up with the sense I was faking it and not capable enough. As my anxiousness grew, my confidence plummeted. The sense that I was not good enough became a constant companion and made it difficult, nearly impossible, for me to lead.

My Imposter Syndrome reached a fever pitch when I held the first team meeting after RJ's passing. RJ hosted two large sales meetings a year, and he had an amazing knack of making sure the meetings were energetic, informational, and fun. I looked in RJ's office for his notes, maybe scraps of ideas that would lead me in the right direction to cobble the meeting together. I found nothing. I was confident in nothing.

It was all on me to create the agenda, schedule the

speakers, reserve the dinners, and plan the outings. My perfectionism, people pleasing, and Imposter Syndrome were spinning out of control because I compared every decision against what RJ had done in the past. I put no stock or confidence in my skills in creating an event designed by me.

The team applauded my effort and the outcome. They said the meeting was a wild success. I was thankful because I did not have confidence in myself. As I delivered the closing speech, tears welled up and my voice cracked, and many team members cried too. It was a cathartic conclusion to RJ's passing and to the event.

Carrying the burden of Imposter Syndrome, every moment of every day, is exhausting. I worked non-stop to prove I was enough and that I could fill RJ's shoes; and this harmed my health. I ignored the signs of exhaustion and burnout because I was only thirty years old. I was young, I could handle it.

After another long week and a ridiculously long day, I fainted in my kitchen. John was out of town, and I was alone with our puppy, Jake. I was surprised to awaken prone on the cold-tile floor to Jake's wet kisses. I don't remember falling. I was lucky that I didn't bash my head on the counter on the way down.

It is amazing what it takes for us to acknowledge our

reality, what we are doing to ourselves, our bodies, and our minds. For me, it was a dog licking my face after collapsing. I missed time; I had no memory of the collapse. I rolled onto my back, stared at the ceiling, and shooed Jake away. *What was I doing? What was happening to me?* I had to take better care of myself. I had to reclaim my confidence, shut down the nasty inner voice, and accept and exude the mantle of leadership that was now mine to wield.

I began taking small steps to rebuild my confidence. Small, but meaningful actions. Instead of looking at how RJ did something, I decided I would do it my way. Instead of getting flustered when people asked if this is how RJ would do it, I responded with, "I am not sure, but this is the way we will do it now." I embraced leading the team authentically and began to leave the Imposter Syndrome behind.

I was confidently leading the team, yet there was still no pay increase or title change. There were no discussions with the CEO about title and pay because I believed that doing the work would speak for itself. Big mistake.

Talent review rolled around, and I was not asked to participate and give feedback on the team members I was leading. Talent review is a process where the leaders of an organization discuss succession planning and high-potential employees, deciding who has a future in leadership at the company. When RJ was alive, he told me the management team didn't see me as leadership material. They didn't think I had it in me. RJ fought for me and went so far to say that I could be the CEO of the organization one day, that is how good I was. With RJ out of the talent review session, and me not included, I wondered how I fared even with me effectively leading the department for over a year. Being excluded raised doubts, which fed into my Imposter Syndrome and almost became a self-fulfilling prophecy.

Eighteen months after RJ passed, my emotional and leadership stores were depleted. I was used by management, exhausted from trying to fill RJ's shoes with no training, mentoring, or support to ensure my organization was thriving. One day, I was asked to interview some dude named Eric, with no information about what role he was interviewing for. I got the distinct feeling that Eric was to be RJ's replacement. That night, I came home and told John, "I think I just interviewed my new boss."

Sure enough, two weeks later, the announcement was made, and Eric was leading the department. I was done. I was angry, frustrated, and hurt. After eighteen months, with no discussion, I had to own that. It was a huge lesson for me. I could not let things go unsaid. I had to find confidence and boldness to let leaders know where

I was at, what I needed, and what my goals were. I was betrayed, but I was not surprised. My confidence was in pieces, but I would not let this define me. I planned and started executing my departure. I networked and sent out resumes immediately.

As I interviewed for different jobs, my confidence grew with each new opportunity. It was oxygen to my soul to look outside of the toxic work environment. I was recruited and hired not for a manager position, nor a director position, nor even an associate director position, but a vice-president's role. Yes, that's right; I jumped from being a throw-away pseudo-manager within an organization that believed I had no potential—to being a vice-president at a company who were ecstatic to have me join their team.

Even though my company didn't appreciate or believe in me, the industry knew what I was doing, the success of the team I was leading, and that I had the experience and capabilities for a larger role. I not only replaced a legend; I became a legend. The new company saw my potential, and I began to see the potential in myself.

I submitted my resignation with trepidation that I was letting the organization, my team, and my friends down. Even on my last day as everyone left early for my going away party, I stayed behind in my office, writing procedures, organizing files, and trying to prove that I was capable. When I walked out the door for the final time, I cried because it was a death to that team, our friendships, and way of life, but it was a birth to the new me.

A few months later, I ran into the CEO and the leadership team from that company at an industry function. It felt good when they told me, "We always knew that you had it in you," even though I felt they were lying. Their fake smug grins and their smarmy style betrayed who they were. I wasn't leadership material for their organization, I was better. They had eighteen months to either give me the role, train or support me, none of which occurred. I nodded in response with my own knowing grin. I was happy that the company was in my rearview mirror. I needed to leave the organization to show everyone, including myself, that I had the confidence, the ability, and the strength to lead.

After the conversation with the CEO and the VPs that day, the imposter voice took a long overdue break. Now, when Imposter Syndrome comes around, I know what to look for and how to handle it. I've learned that Imposter Syndrome is the voice of fear and is simply there to do its job of protecting me. Then I let the imposter voice know that I'm thankful for its work, but that it needs to take a back seat and let me drive.

I lead now through challenging situations and trying new things, and I'm not crippled by doubt, fear, or lack of confidence. It took many years for me to learn this, and I'm proud that I've made it this far. Of course, I am still working on it, because that is what we do on our journey to be our full and confident selves.

After taking time to reflect, I learned that I have a different personality and leadership style than RJ, and that is OK. Anytime we try to mirror someone else, we set ourselves up for failure. This is a big reason for my bout with Imposter Syndrome. I was trying to be someone I wasn't. As soon as I fully owned my gifts, strengths, and experience, I confidently became the leader that I was meant to be.

Do not wait for others to tell you that you are a leader. Confidence to lead must come from within. What if I believed the results of the talent reviews? If I waited for my former employer to tell me that I was ready for a leadership role, I would still be waiting.

Here are some key lessons I learned about myself and confidence building through RJ's passing, my interim responsibilities, and my struggles with Imposter Syndrome:

- **Don't ignore the red flags and take personal responsibility.**

I ignored the fact that I was in a toxic work environment. In addition, I overlooked the reality that I was doing the work of two people after RJ's passing without the title or the pay. I erroneously believed I needed to uphold RJ's legacy and do some imaginary right thing for the team. Unfortunately, I now realize that the organization and my team preyed on my lack of self-confidence. They allowed, even encouraged, me to work countless hours, sacrifice time with my family, and put my health in jeopardy for eighteen months for their own benefit.

I let that happen. I take personal responsibility for allowing this set of circumstances to continue for so long. I stayed in a toxic work environment. I took on the unnecessary burden of responsibility after RJ's passing. I allowed the organization to let me languish without the commensurate title and pay, or even support and guidance. I did that. And I now know better.

- **Listen to your own intuition and desire, and not the naysayers.**

  Listen to your intuition and not the negative thoughts from others. The leaders at that company had no idea what I could do, but I did. I knew I could do more.

Listen to the still and powerful wisdom inside. It will serve you well and get you to where you need to go much faster. I waited too long to know this; don't wait as long as I did.

- **Take small steps.**
You can find your confidence by taking small steps each day. Speak up at a meeting. Ask the question. Say no when you mean it. Set and hold a boundary. These small actions stack up and grow your confidence and leadership muscle. This prepares you for taking larger and bolder actions when needed.

- **Recognize it takes time.**
Building self-confidence doesn't happen overnight. It takes time for confidence to grow and blossom. There are times when you take one step forward and two steps back. It is part of the process, and that's OK.

- **Celebrate your wins.**
Don't let the Imposter Syndrome, perfectionism, people pleasing, or anything else steal the joy from your wins. Having the confidence to lead is difficult but so worth it. Take the time to celebrate as you invest in your confidence and forge your path.

- **Know your boundaries and recognize when they are crossed.**

  First, define your boundaries. Spend time exploring what is non-negotiable. What behaviors or actions will you not tolerate? Then evaluate what is occurring around you; this requires routine and constant reflection. Ask a mentor or a trusted colleague to give you honest feedback. An outside source is often required to help you see what is happening.

- **Negotiate, negotiate, negotiate.**

  If you are not satisfied with the compensation, title, or benefits in your role, negotiate. Ask the question, "Can we discuss my compensation?" or "Can we discuss my work schedule or (*enter benefit here*)?" You must state your desires; how else will they know? I assure you that working hard and assuming someone will recognize and compensate you for it is likely to never happen. Worst case scenario: they say no. Then you are armed with information and can decide if you want to continue with the company. Either way, have the confidence and self-respect to garner the pay, title, and benefits that you deserve. You are worth it and deserve it.

- **Don't settle.**

  This is a tough one for me. I get comfortable in jobs and patterns and am uncomfortable with change. Does this resonate with you? If so, don't get too comfortable and don't settle for a second-best career or life. We often get comfy with our routines. We don't spend enough time reflecting. I challenge you to answer these questions at least annually:

  - Am I in a professional environment where I'm thriving? If so, how?
  - If not, what changes do I need to make?
  - What do I need to move forward personally or professionally?

If you find that you are not in a position or place where you are thriving, think about the changes you need to make to get on the right path once again. And remember, sometimes you will take one step forward and two steps back on your journey towards confidence and progress. It may be uncomfortable or even scary, but no matter what happens, it's always better than settling.

*"Whether you think you can, or think
you can't, you're right."*
—Henry Ford

INTRODUCING DR. ZENOBIA TANTRA

Dr. Zenobia Tantra, or Dr. Zen as her patients call her, is a Doctor of Physical Therapy with a specialty in male and female pelvic floor healing from conception to menopause and beyond. She was trained and educated at the University of Illinois at Chicago, Rosalind Franklin University and did her rotations at the University of Chicago, Copley in Aurora, which is affiliated with Rush, and at the Chicago Institute of Neurosurgery and Neuroresearch. She has her Pelvic Floor certification from the APTA.

Dr. Zen combines her knowledge of Western and Eastern modalities, including traditional pelvic floor therapy, energy medicine, and complementary alternative medicine, at her clinical practice Zenxuality to empower her clients to heal themselves.

Using her training from the Benson Henry Institute and Harvard Medical School in Mind-Body Medicine,

Hormone Management, and the years of Chakra, Tantra and Kama Sutra tutelage and wisdom, she customizes each plan for the healing journey with an emphasis on privacy, safety, respect, and consent.

Through her work at Zenxuality, she helps her patients reach their highest levels of Spirituality, Sensuality, and Sexuality through what she calls the cradle of life, our pelvic floors. Dr. Zen focuses on physically and energetically cleansing and clearing blockages, pain, and the energy centers involved, to enable her patients to become their most royal and powerful selves.

Dr. Zen exudes passion, energy, joy and celebrates life. She aspires to empower her clients and enable them to embrace their health, positivity, sexuality, happiness, and well-being.

Zenobia enjoys sacred love, affirmations, reading, learning, meditation, yoga, traveling, teaching, dancing, volunteering, exquisite culinary experiences (basically she is a foodie), and spending time with her beautiful family and friends.

CONFIDENCE: OUR SHINING JEWEL

"Self-confidence is self-respect."
—Sri Govindu

"A woman is unstoppable once she loves and embraces herself and has her own self-approval. Now, that is the ultimate confidence."
—Dr. Zenobia Tantra

Words are powerful. A good quote elevates, excites and sets my heart a-flutter and my jewel shining bright. When words cut and debase, they start a storm within our chests. Torrential weather in your chest is one of the quickest ways for your jewel to dim and your confidence to be shaken or betrayed. Words.

"What have you done? You are so insecure," he declared. Words like these put a dagger through your heart and shake your confidence and are even more hurtful when they come from someone you love, care about, and respect. I was left with a gaping hole in my heart. This was my best friend and partner. I have big emotions. I was born and raised an Indian and my ethnicity and heritage is Persian. Emotions are in my blood. Emotion is energy in motion, and his words tsunamied through me. It was a personal earthquake, tsunami, and a tornado, all rolled into one. Especially since I was asked this question after twenty years of helping build a company from scratch, from being the senator to the janitor. Caring for the company like my own baby.

I was asked this question after being the backbone that built the business, playing every role needed to ensure the company succeeded. And with that phrase, the wind was taken out of my sails, all my achievements slipped away in a wash of words. I felt insecure, though the evidence of my performance contradicted any reason for me to feel this way. But there I was, letting the words and the opinions of others define me. This is when you realize the value of confidence.

Let's explore the meaning of the word, "confidence." My dear friend Hosi is big on word play and knows that words are powerful, and their meaning and use is important. He is one of my many teachers and has turned me onto the simple wisdom and power of words. Words can enhance or diminish a connection with others and even within ourselves. I look at words and seek their deeper meaning and wisdom. It is within us to build a foundation of confidence that cannot be uprooted. And in that moment, inspiring words came to me, guiding my exit from that season of my life.

Confidence, according to me, is the ability to confide in yourself and in the people you love and trust. When someone you love and trust violates it, the venom of betrayal hurts even more.

I believe that I am responsible for myself. I believe in myself. Regardless of what others say, or scream, at me, I am responsible to do the work to improve my confidence and my being. If we cannot trust and confide in ourselves then everything else is superfluous and we let external elements control us. We lose the ability to stand up for and believe in ourselves.

This was the start of my journey in building unshakable confidence, finding my love of quotes to inspire me, creating my own brand, and to lift up others in everything I do, no matter the outcome. I am a self-proclaimed, self-professed quotaholic (yes, I made up that word). I adore quotes, not only because they provide wisdom, inspiration, and guidance; but selected quotes are a window into one's psyche, one's soul, and true beliefs and value systems. Quotes also give us a glimpse into different cultures, philosophies, and civilizations.

This brings me back to the quote I thought of at that moment when I was betrayed and crying: "No one can make you feel inferior without your consent." Brilliant Mrs. Eleanor Roosevelt knew what she was talking about.

Why give anyone that power over you? Through tears and sobs and while yelling and screaming, I thought of this quote, lifted my chin, declared my worth and value, and then walked out of the room. Even though I was still crying and hurting, I was now doing it on my time and on my terms.

This is when I needed my Manipura, my Solar Plexus-Navel Chakra, to see me through and shine brightly. Manipura, in the Sanskrit language, means a Lustrous Gem, a Shining Jewel.

The words that were hurled at me left me ravaged, and I needed all the Manipura shine, power, and help that I could get. I would process the events then bounce back stronger, like I always do. It takes work and clarity of focus to return to our confident selves. We must give ourselves grace and understand that it takes time, but our power is in the knowing. Knowing we will return. I always return to myself.

Some of my friends and patients call me POP—Princess of Positivity. Some compare me to Dory in Finding Nemo, because no matter what, I keep on swimming and going forward. I refuse to let others jade my Pollyanna view of our beautiful world and the Universe. An all-time favorite quote is by Dr. Wayne Dyer, may his soul continue in eternal bliss, "How people treat you is their Karma, how you react to them, is yours."

My culture, upbringing and value system have established such a powerful connection to the energy that we are all blessed with, the energy in our chakras—our direct connection to our creator and the power bestowed upon us when brought to this Earth, to heal and strengthen ourselves, and to serve those around us. I am humbled and honored to be of Persian ancestry and of Indian heritage; my growth and knowledge started in my lovely culture through prayer and energy-focused awareness and growth.

Zoroastrianism teaches us that our life is guided by Humata, Hukhta, Hvarshta, which means Good Thoughts, Good Words, Good Deeds. It further teaches us that we are the captains of our souls and the masters of our destiny.

There is power in that statement. You have the power to create your best life by using the best words for you. I pray daily to reinforce this. Some chant. Some sing. Some read aloud. Some envision powerful words in their mind, heart, and body. The physical and energy work that I do daily reinforces this notion to nourish souls and bodies to be strong, sound, and confident.

My daily prayer of Yatha Ahu Vairyo strengthens this. The energy work that I do daily nourishes my soul, mind, and body. Yatha Ahu Vairyo, one of my all-time favorites and most used prayer, bestows the message that, "I must revere Ahura Mazda (God) and that I must appraise and assimilate his Asha (Truth), Righteousness, and Order and practice it in my daily life. I must perform selfless deeds so that I develop Wisdom, Virtue, and Love. I must help others in need so that I receive and develop the inner strength, power and confidence to do more and more good." Sometimes the simplest way to not stay lost in a lack of confidence is by serving others. It is the fastest way to fill up our cups, both ours and theirs, with this wisdom and God-given energy in action.

Manipura, our Third Chakra, our Solar Plexus-Navel Chakra is our powerhouse. It is a source of centering, hope, and confidence. It is all about self-esteem and asserting ourselves in a positive way. Energy work on our Third Chakra builds our self-esteem, our hope and our confidence and enables us to assert ourselves in a positive way. I repeat this to bring home the message of the power of energy work. The name Manipura itself means a "Lustrous Gem, a Shining Jewel," always the jewel of which I speak.

Who are we then to defy God, the Universe and Energy, and be any less than glowing in our unique light? When we let others define our worth and our value, we are defying the divine plan for our lives and ourselves. We would be wise to let the energy of the Universe flow through and empower ourselves. When we are our full confident selves, we allow others around us to also be their full selves.

I believe that confidence, just like happiness, is an inside job. How else can we confide in ourselves and emerge vulnerable, yet strong? How else can we be authentic while maintaining our strength and integrity? Our personal jewel, at the center of our creation, grounds and guides us, if we nourish it properly.

My ancestry and upbringing led me to a destiny to help everyone's root chakra, physically and mentally, clearing what's needed to get people to their fullest, most powerful presence in life. I was blessed by so many examples in my shaping, my family, my culture, my heritage, my teachers, and much more to help my jewel shine the brightest.

Growing up in a one-hundred-and-thirty-square-foot

apartment with my parents and sister in Mumbai, India, I always dreamt of coming to the U. S. I imagined The United States would be like the *David Copperfield* book by Charles Dickens, where the streets of London were paved in gold. The beautiful U. S. A. was the land of opportunity and possibility, and where, if you worked hard and persisted, you were unstoppable.

My father was only able to finish high school, and my mother had to drop out of school by the sixth grade due to financial hardship; but they instilled the value of a good education in me. My Keku Kakaji (grand uncle), Minoo Kakaji (grand uncle), and Jamshed Mamaji (Grand uncle) not only encouraged education but were also living examples of hard work, brilliance, loyalty, and unconditional love and generosity.

They were my superheroes, my role models—may their beautiful souls continue in eternal bliss. Having this generational support helped me to realize my dreams and to become confident enough to take important leaps needed to be here sharing this American Dream, realized with all of you beautiful souls.

All this played a role in molding me and shaping my confidence as I realized that not even the sky was the limit as there are footprints on the moon. Bollywood and Disney movies further solidified my limitless outlook.

They created magical worlds where anything was possible. I was told by well-meaning friends of my parents and by other relatives, that my dad was not able to afford train fare from Mumbai to Andheri, and here I was planning and talking about going to America.

As I grew up, Bollywood, the Hindi film industry, was a part of my life and provided an escape into all things romantic, sometimes silly, and always magical. The movies were inspirational and motivational, and their awe-inspiring theatrics made my dreams and the potential for magic come to life for me in my childhood and youth. In these worlds, anything was possible. I escaped into worlds full of strength, hope, and possibility.

I learned about the essence of life through the movie *Anand*, with the late and great Mr. Rajesh Khanna: "*Babu Moshai, Zindagi badi honi chahiye, lambi nahi,*" which means, "Life needs to be big in the way you live it; longevity does not correlate to greatness, achievement, and generosity."

Superstar Mr. Shahrukh Khan's movie *Baazigar* brought home the message that one must keep trying to truly win. Failure is the steppingstone to success. The dialogue goes, "*Haar kar jeetne waale ko hi Baazigar kehte hai,*" which means "The one who fails and keeps trying and then wins is the true winner."

My all-time favorite quote on confidence has been the one by the gorgeous and talented Mrs. Kareena Kapoor Khan in the movie *Jab We Met* which says, *"Main apni favorite hoon,"* meaning, to the point, "I am my favorite." This to me is the ultimate epitome of acceptance, authenticity, vulnerability, and confidence.

My Hindi film industry tribute and influence is incomplete without the mention of the iconic and all-time favorite superstar and gentleman, Mr. Amitabh Bachchan—the man, the legend. I grew up watching his movies; and his voice, command of the language, aura, and energy are in a class and league of their own.

In the 1981 movie *Kaalia,* an inmate displays confidence when he says, *"Hum bhi vo hai jo kabhi kisi ke peeche nahi khade hote..... jaha khade ho jate hai, line wahi se shuru hoti hai,"* which means "I am also the one that does not stand behind anyone else and the line begins from where I stand." The difference here is that he does not use his power to bully, but to stand up to the bullies of the world. In the movie scene, he confidently stands up to the bully by stepping in and removing the bully's power, stoically and powerfully. He states that he will not be intimidated, he will not be made inferior. In this scene, he is not only standing up for himself, but for others. He demonstrates our duty to stand up for those that need help. The ability to exude power and confidence to help others is noble and right. Confidence is also about standing up for those that are unable to do so for themselves.

Finally, confidence at its best is displayed in the movie *Queen* in which the brilliant and beautiful Ms. Kangana Ranaut plays the role of a Punjabi girl who, when jilted by her fiancé, instead of retreating and being subject to taunts and gossip, embarks on her singlemoon (honeymoon by herself) to Europe. She explores, learns, and lives fully unto herself. This is confidence: a story of hope, triumph, belief, and confidence in oneself and in self-discovery. In recent times, *Gangubai Kathiawadi* is epic and to me the actress is a poster child for confidence. It is about a beautiful young girl, Ganga, who is lured to Mumbai from her hometown by her boyfriend on the false promise of a career in the Hindi film industry. It is a "real-life tale of an Indian activist born into brothel culture who went on to become a notable social crusader." The talented and stunning Mrs. Alia Bhatt-Kapoor oozes confidence and makes you want to cry, cheer, and rally for her throughout the film. To me it has become a "go to" for a confidence surge as almost every reel of the film with Gangubai displays confidence in one form or the other.

There are several dialogues that are praiseworthy and inspirational and my all-time favorite that exemplifies confidence is, "*Arey, jab Shakti, Sampatti aur Sadhbuddhi, yeh teeno hi aurtein hai, toh in mardo ko kiss baat ka guroor?*" The meaning of the above words is that "When Strength, Wealth, and Intelligence are all Female Goddesses and embody feminine qualities, then what do the men have to be egotistical and arrogant about?" Well, Beautiful Ladies, please keep that in your arsenal, because you truly have it all: Strength, Intelligence, and the ability and power to generate wealth.

Though well-intentioned advisors told me that my dreams were out of reach, I chose to live within the magic and the dream, and my faith in God—and I prayed. Being a firm believer in God and the Universe, and knowing that magic happens, I continued to believe and put energy into the manifestation of my dreams. My Manipura led me with steps of confidence, with persistence, and consistent belief. I believed and manifested. Thirteen years later, my roots were replanted in the amazing United States of America where eventually the Zenobia Goddess in me would arise and thrive.

I was nineteen years old, and my feet were standing on U. S. soil. Zubin, my husband, supported my dreams and helped me come here for higher education. He is a tireless supporter and my soul's partner. He is the wind beneath my wings. This was made possible because of

God and the Universe, love, and energy manifestation. The answer to my prayers, and all the Bollywood magic in the world could never come close to describing my journey into his arms and our life together.

My given name is Zenobia, and I married a man named Zubin Tantra, making me who I was born to be through this union—Dr. Zen Tantra. I think this is better than any movie I've ever seen; me—living this dream! I am forever grateful to my husband for encouraging me, supporting me, and for making it possible for me to continue my studies in the land paved with Golden Dreams: The United States of America. I attended the University of Illinois at Chicago for a bachelor's in physical therapy, proceeded to obtain a specialization in Pelvic Floor Rehabilitation through the American Physical Therapy Association, and secured a post-professional doctorate through Chicago Medical School, now named Rosalind Franklin University. I did rotations at some of the best institutions in the Chicagoland area and traveled the world to learn from the best and the greatest. I continue to learn and seek.

When I was asked, "What have you done?" "You are so insecure," I thought of the impactful *Gangubai*, quote *"Arey, jab Shakti, Sampatti aur Sadhbuddhi, yeh teeno hi aurtein hai, toh in mardo ko kiss baat ka guroor?"* I humbly reiterate the meaning that, "When Strength, Wealth, and Intelligence are all Female Goddesses and embody feminine qualities, then what do the men have to be egotistical and arrogant about?" To answer those hurtful questions, the Gangubai in me emerged and raised her head and started shining my Manipura to realize that I had nothing to prove and that I am enough.

Strength, wealth, and intelligence are all female energy and goddesses, and it is about time that we accept and claim our crown. In that moment, it was past time that I claimed my throne and realized my worth and potential. This statement blesses me with the basis of who I am as a woman and empowers me to show other women who they are too. It's time to embrace and claim our throne. We are worthy.

This professional loss was also my breakthrough as it encouraged me and led to the initiation of my own business. I took the leap of faith and founded my own healthcare company: Zenxuality, where Spirituality, Sensuality, and Sexuality merge to unleash the Goddess and Powerhouse in All of Us.

This is my Purpose, my Dharma, my way to serve others. Where all my healing training—radical positivity, zest for life, chakra energy renewal training, quotes to inspire, physical therapy, kama sutra, tantra, and pelvic floor specialty education and more—helps men and women reach their highest levels of Spirituality, Sensuality and Sexuality through the cradle of life. I call the Pelvic Floor, the cradle of civilization, because, if there were no pelvic floors, none of us would be here.

My patients and I begin work with our root chakra and proceed through the physical and spiritual chakras to align us into our royal, most powerful selves. I had been working on patients and clients with energy work in Pelvic Floor Rehabilitation for years, and it was now time to own it.

Starting a company is fun, scary—a true test of perseverance, belief in self, and confidence. But like the saying goes, "No Guts. No Glory." It is built on confidence and the knowledge that failure will come but must be followed by learning and perseverance. Time to follow the power of my Manipura, keep shining it, and blaze forward fearlessly. It is an honor to make the health and energy of men and women shine their brightest through my work and business, where I've also found the most powerful Goddess within myself. I used this opportunity to continue learning and incorporating alternative and holistic practices to empower the amazing souls I had the honor to work with, with a wholistic (as we look at the whole picture) approach.

My children are my teachers, mentors, and my mirror.

They have taught me valuable lessons and continue to do so. My son, Zayden when he was seven years old, introduced himself to his new teacher and told her that even though he was starting second grade he was already doing fourth grade math. He clarified that he was not bragging, he was letting her know that he needed a challenge. Wow! Talk about confidence.

My daughter, Zaara, is my Zoda. We call her Zoda because she reminds us of Yoda with her wisdom and poise. At three-and-a-half years of age, she told me that she was not from planet Earth and that she was shy when she met people for the first time but was more comfortable with them once she got to interact with them and got to know them. At five-and-a-half, she reminded me that not only was she not from Mother Earth, but she was also not from the Milky Way galaxy. She did it with confidence, poise, and with a matter-of-fact attitude. She built on it at seven years of age saying that her shyness had nothing to do with confidence as she knew that she was amazing and enough.

At nine years old, she told me that confidence is about courage and self-pride. Self-pride in herself and about herself. That, even though she may not always feel confident, she just believes in herself and shows up. Wow! I want to be like that when I grow up. I wanted her to write this chapter. She comes up with the best quotes to keep us aligned to what is gifted to each of us at such a young age, and she magically maintains it.

The Manipura development stage is from eighteen months to four years. After this, we must keep reminding ourselves of our shine, to polish our jewel, and that our power is infinite as sometimes our internal voice attempts to sabotage us as we continue to struggle with our inner self and the world.

I maintain that many of us have made great strides in our external facing worlds and in outer space, but for many of us, our inner world is still bereft and lacking due to our own self-imposed limitations. Our inner world needs exploration, growth, and understanding. Every person is beautiful and enough in their own way, yet as women we always feel the need to prove ourselves and seek external validation.

We can be stunningly dressed, brilliant and charming, own the room and the audience, but deep down, we tend to have our insecurities and our doubts, our fears, and our hesitation which sometimes leads to second guessing, self-flagellation, and minimizing our greatness. It is common for us to seek external validation to prove our worth. Manipura Chakra energy work gently reminds us that, "It is not power we seek so much as the overcoming of victimization—the ability to determine our own lives." I take it a step further and say, if something is not aligned, let us get to the root of the imbalance and shift into shining brighter. Shall we?

"For what greater responsibility than to allow the divine within, the freedom of its unique unfoldment?"
—**Anodea Judith**

Which takes me to a quote, source unknown, that sits in my bathroom, and I read it every day. It says, "The woman that does not require validation from anyone is the most feared individual on the planet." To this I say, let us work on our will and our choices, let us accept our greatness and let it shine through.

Manipura is a dynamic light, about fire and will. We all have the power and shine within us. The above quote reignites my purpose to help all with accepting this amazing gift. Let us make our shine the brightest it can be to use it for the greater good. Like the late and great Mahatma Gandhiji said, "Be the change that you want to see in the world."

I start with myself and spread the glow as I grow. Our confidence is like a muscle. We keep working on it and developing it with humility, humor, and grace. When I was asked to be a part of this project, I understood this was an opportunity for me to share knowledge, techniques, and reassurance for people traveling on their journeys to confidence. Confidence building requires focused energy and trust in our innate power.

I have learned from life—and my daughter, Zaara, reinforces it—that it is alright to make mistakes. I always say that as long as we are learning and growing from them, we are moving upward and forward. My children and I were playing a game at home when my son exclaimed, "We won!" He and Zaara were on the same team. My daughter looked at me and said, "You win, and you learn, you win, and you have fun. There is no such thing as losing if you are learning from it." I keep that message close to my heart when my confidence needs a gentle boost. It is all about learning and growing, as the more I live the more I realize that I don't know anything and that I have a lot to learn. This is not a lack of confidence but an awareness of the infinite possibilities. We should all be open and not closed to that notion.

"Scared is what happens when the Sacred gets scrambled."
—**Anodea Judith**

When you bring your unique shining light into any conversation, job, relationship, or project, you lay the groundwork for your confidence to grow and for it to inspire growth in others. It is a significant introspective journey that must be taken. Some will get through it quickly and effortlessly; others are more deliberate and specific about each step in the learning process. The timing is individual and just the act of doing it is a significant achievement. Acknowledge and celebrate every moment in this journey that ends in unshakable confidence. There are many eras and experiences that shaped mine. I am excited and grateful to share my journey with you. I hope it helps your unique jewel to shine the brightest.

"Do not live in fear. Determine your sacred connection to confidence and make it second nature."
—**Dr. Zenobia Tantra**

Remembering what the amazing Mrs. Eleanor Roosevelt quoted, I walked out of that room forever changed. I had briefly consented in that moment by feeling worthless at someone's words that shifted me professionally, but I took power back in the moment and in each moment following. I am building myself into a woman discovering which words to use, to say to herself and to say aloud to make sure she always knows she is strong and safe, and no one determines her value but her. A confident woman, a woman who goes beyond words to find her strength to be the most powerful version of herself to best serve others and be a force to reckon with. This is confidence, not arrogance. Words and Energy matter. Choose Wisely!

Dear reader, thank you for sharing your precious time with me. I send and share with you my light, my love, my joy, my gratitude, and my confidence. I sincerely hope that you shine bright as you travel your beautiful journey and adventure called life.

In parting, I bequeath you this amazing chant from the *Bhagavad Gita*:

When you don't believe in yourself, you lose your Confidence.

When you lose Confidence, you look for others' approval.

As soon as you look for others' approval, you lose your Self-respect.

"Self-Confidence is Self-Respect."
—**Sri Govindu**

Keep Your Confidence, your Crown, and your Energy intact. May the light and the energy of the Universe flow through you. Thank You. Namaste! Yatha!

EPILOGUE

As the managing editor, I engage with each author, each chapter, and each submission individually and holistically. Each piece evolves and improves throughout the process while the contributing author gains confidence and comfort with the submitted chapter. I am humbled and honored to serve in this capacity for the incredible women of the Brave Women at Work community. It also means that I see common threads within their works.

This is a book about confidence—gaining and growing confidence—however with the first round of submissions not a single author included the word *promoted*. Each of these authors is well established, has had big jobs, and big lives and has moved through a series of promotions. Not one of them called it that. They contorted their words and their submissions to find alternate ways to say, "I was promoted." It is so ingrained in us not to be boastful or overly confident that within a book on confidence no one was promoted. You will find the word included now, not too much, but acknowledging promotions is important and calling them that is OK too; it is not bragging or arrogant, it is simply what happened. *I was promoted.* Be encouraged to use strong and real language to reflect the accomplishments in your life.

Several submissions included the concept of hiding or reducing themselves at different periods in their lives and careers. We hid from our fears, our promotions, our challenges, and sometimes we hid from ourselves. We made ourselves smaller and less significant to fit the mold or expectations of others. Each author discovered this method did not serve them and did not help them on their journey with confidence. There is no benefit or joy in shrinking yourself to make others comfortable. We each must step fully into our authentic selves and not reduce ourselves nor our contributions to realize and embrace confidence.

We also learned that many carry an outward appearance of confidence, but internally struggle with anxiety and self-doubt. We arm ourselves, dress the part, do our hair and make-up, then try not to puke before we speak at a podium. The colleague you have been jealous of for years may be questioning his or her own worth and value while you think they are strong and confident. This correlates to the concept of grace.

Our authors discovered that we are often willing and eager to grant grace to our friends, colleagues, and family members, while granting ourselves a measure of grace is more difficult. We must unlearn the habit of beating ourselves up for mistakes. Mistakes and failures are required for success. With each failure or challenge we overcome; our confidence grows. We know we can do it. We know that no matter what we face we will be able to work the problem, find a solution; and being graceful with ourselves gives room for that knowledge and confidence.

Each author deployed different methods to find her own confidence. Some used mantras, some used networks, some used a check list, and others dreamed big and dismissed the naysayers along the way. Some had to realize what they did not want in order to take the initial steps in finding their confidence. Many stacked up educational milestones which bolstered and developed their confidence and self-identification. No matter how they got there, it is clear that confidence is an internal job. Confidence cannot be built or maintained from external sources. We must believe in and love ourselves first, and from that our confidence blooms.

BOOK CLUB DISCUSSION GUIDE

Why not me?

1. What would you do or say if you were guaranteed success?

2. What do your gremlins tell you? Gremlins are the critical voices in our head that can sabotage our self-confidence; e. g., *I am not smart enough.*

3. What is holding you back? Are these skills that you can hone? If so, what are you doing to act on them?

4. What do you want to ask for, but are afraid to? *Why not you?*

Reanimation

1. What was the biggest contributor to the author's ability to regain confidence and what surprised you about any of her steps taken?

2. How often are we surrounded by high performers who struggle with losing themselves and their confidence in our own workplaces today? How can we help them?

3. The author speaks of finding a new sense of purpose through crisis which then sparks additional opportunities. How has a crisis launched you into action instead of defeat?

The Knowing Within

1. To what extent does your confidence level correlate with your sense of identity?

2. How have your early development experiences influenced your level of confidence?

3. How does your connection to purpose and personal values relate to your confidence level?

You are More

1. Are you on your own journey or are you living by someone else's rules or expectations for you?

2. Do you struggle with negative self-talk? What steps can you take to stop negative self-talk?

3. What steps are you willing to take to help grow your confidence and courage?

Anxious Over-Achiever

1. What steps do you take when you notice that you have high levels of stress or anxiety?
2. What factors or influences, if any, from your early childhood years have affected your confidence level in the workplace?
3. What factors about your work environment or employer contribute to low self-confidence? Do any of these factors cause you to overcompensate like the author?
4. What have you found helps you build your self-confidence?

I've Got This!

1. What word or phrase do you have that reminds you to trust your abilities?
2. What do you do when you notice your confidence shifting whether in your work or personal life?
3. Share a time that you made a change—whether it be a job, career, or life change—that impacted your confidence. Looking back on that time now, what do you wish you knew to prepare for? What could you have done differently to be prepared for the impact?

Imposter

1. Have you experienced Imposter Syndrome? What were your symptoms, and how did it impact your professional or personal life?
2. After reading this chapter, what steps will you take to manage bouts with Imposter Syndrome moving forward?
3. What are some signs to watch out for to ensure that your hard work and dedication are not taken for granted at work?
4. Have you ever put your head down and worked very hard in hopes of a promotion but were passed up for the opportunity? What was the outcome, and what did you learn?

Confidence: Our Shining Jewel

1. We all experience a lack of confidence at different times of our lives. What do you use to get over the hurdle and bounce back?
2. Describe your support system.
3. How do you keep your Manipura and Crown shining bright?

ACKNOWLEDGEMENTS— JENNIFER PESTIKAS

I would like to start by thanking Hope Mueller, who continues to listen to and encourage my crazy, big ideas. I love the journey we are traveling together. Hope is an amazing teacher, mentor, and friend. I look forward to partnering with Hope on many projects in the years to come.

Thank you to the contributing authors from my previous work *Brave Women at Work: Stories of Resilience* for your ongoing support and encouragement. Having you part of my world is a wonderful blessing.

Thank you to the contributing authors from *Brave Women at Work: Lessons in Confidence* for your passion and dedication to the book creation process.

To the readers, followers, and members of the Brave Women at Work community, your willingness to participate in this group of amazing women is awe-inspiring. I am grateful for you, and it is for you that I do this work.

I would like to thank my beautiful daughters, Charlotte and Olivia Pestikas. Charlotte, you forever changed my world in the most wonderful way when I became your mama. Olivia, thank you for the joy and light you bring to our lives. You remind me to appreciate each moment of love and laughter we share together.

Thank you to my niece, Abby Lemon. It was a joy to see your face during the *Brave Women at Work: Stories of Resilience* book signing. It was full of power and possibility. I love you, Abby, and want you to know you can do anything you put your heart and mind to.

To my mom, Gail Lemon: You have been one of my biggest cheerleaders and counselors throughout my career. Thank you for always giving it to me straight and loving me through it all.

And to my husband, John Pestikas: I appreciate your support and encouragement of my dream to help women get the education and inspiration they need to take braver and bolder action in their careers. I love you!

ACKNOWLEDGMENTS— HOPE MUELLER

Jennifer Pestikas and I have entered a journey together happily titled "naïve joy." When we launched *Brave Women at Work: Stories of Resilience,* neither one of us had been part of or published an anthology before. This second book in the series, *Brave Women at Work: Lessons in Confidence,* was much more organized to compose and we learned a lot, again. We launched into another "naïve joy" effort—designing, hosting, and delivering a women's retreat. It was an unmitigated success and a life-changing event for us and our guests. Jennifer and I have a trusting partnership, which is a safe space for us to learn, grow, develop, and push each other to our highest levels. I am thankful she has entered my life and I cannot wait to see what we do together.

I want to recognize Amy Dieschbourg. Amy volunteered to support Jennifer and me in a myriad of ways, allowing me to keep this project a priority while delivering on the women's retreat initiative. Amy moves into a space and owns it. Without question, without pause, Amy is now part of the fabric of Hunter Street Press, Brave Women at Work, and C. L. I. M. B. Conferences. We are endlessly thankful for her help to see these projects come to life.

The contributing authors in *Lessons in Confidence* are a group of incredible women. They were engaged, supportive, and curious. Their chapter submissions were strong, and they are now part of the Brave Women at Work family for life. They join the authors of *Brave Women at Work: Stories of Resilience*, Hunter Street Press authors, and the broader Brave Women at Work community. I continue to be honored and humbled to work amongst such brilliant, confident, and successful women.

Huge thanks to my dedicated readers, followers, and subscribers. Their willingness to purchase, share, like, post, and help promote our projects does not go unnoticed, and without whom all projects would be abject failures. The list is too long to include but please know that I see and appreciate you.

My four daughters, who all show more confidence and aplomb than I did at their respective ages, bring me more joy and pride than could be imagined or adequately described. My two grandsons give my life an unparalleled fulfillment.

Thank you to my mom, Paula Cordes, for your unconditional love which laid the foundation for every measure of success I achieve and enjoy today. Your legacy lies in confident women, resilient women, and women who want to give back to the world.

Thank you, Brad Mueller. Your steadfast love and acceptance of me, and generous support of these projects, is relished. None of this would be possible without your commitment and backing. Let's Do This!

OTHER PUBLICATIONS BY HUNTER STREET PRESS:

Brave Women at Work: Stories of Resilience

Become, a guided inspirational journal

Counting Hope, from conflict to confidence

Hopey, from commune to corner office

First, Only, Different by Shelia Higgs-Burkhalter

I transitioned into new positions, at new institutions, in new cities eight times now. I've done it as an unpartnered single woman, a partnered single woman, a married woman, and with a family in tow. Heck, I was even a contributing author for a book about how to effectively plan and execute a job search and how to manage the transition. As you might imagine, I am skilled at spotting red flags, hearing what's not being said, picking up on underlying messages, and parsing out the backstory when completing the environmental scanning of a new employment opportunity. Sounds intense? Well, it is. After all, making career moves involves my husband of

22 years who is a professional, and a teenaged daughter who has opinions about, well, everything. This journey is not just about making a living; it's about making a life.

I have learned that looking through the rearview mirror focused on where you've been or what you're leaving behind creates a blind spot for seeing what is ahead. I strive to keep my eyes forward with clarity about what I want and need, including a list of my negotiables and non-negotiables. This was absolutely the case in my last job search, or so I thought.

I didn't deign to type a single letter on an application unless the university met some critical criteria. A focus on the student experience, student success, and a visible commitment to diversity, equity, and inclusion (DEI) would be the driving catalyst for a deeper exploration. Visible evidence that an institution was "walking their talk" was a must. Finally, the perks of a vibrant city coupled with the benefits of suburban living, proximity to family, familiarity with the area, and a robust position profile were necessary.

My search led to the identification of what seemed like an ideal opportunity. The vice-president for student affairs opportunity at Winthrop University in Rock Hill, SC appeared to have the right title, the right portfolio, and the right location. It ticked all of the boxes of being the right institution. Check. Check. Check. I applied.

I'd had a series of challenging past work experiences that made me question if I had paid close enough attention or asked the right questions during the selection and interview process. I was hypervigilant about understanding what I required for my next opportunity. Then I conducted validity checks to be sure that I'd recognize it when I found it. I conducted deep environmental scanning by reading any material within arms or virtual reach. I talked with individuals in my network who had knowledge of the institution. I had an action-packed interview experience that included a phone interview, neutral site interview (AKA airport interview) with a committee of 12 people, the provost and president, and a two-and-a-half-day campus experience that included interviews with 75+ individuals and groups. I did solo and guided tours of the campus and city and a realtor tour. I met with a group of 30 students from a wide array of backgrounds and experiences. I even had an off-schedule conversation with a group of Black professionals at various levels of the institution to understand their lived experiences. I developed a three-page single-spaced list of questions and unabashedly asked them all. I wanted to know precisely what I might be walking into if I was offered and accepted this position.

The answers to my questions weren't perfect, but they were open and honest. There were clearly challenges ahead, but nothing I didn't feel prepared to handle. After all, I was a 24-year seasoned professional transitioning from an eight-year chief student affairs role. I understood the sometimes-harsh realities of running a comprehensive institution. I knew the jargon and the hidden meaning behind certain phrases. I knew that a historic campus meant deferred maintenance. I knew that right sizing the institution meant budget reductions. I knew that realigning staffing likely meant permanent elimination of positions. The pros outweighed the cons; the highly relational Southern hospitality and the inclusive, innovative, engaging, and thoughtful interview process drew me in more deeply. The robust offer, the match with my non-negotiable list, the wonderful students, and the spirit of the colleagues with whom I'd be working sealed the deal. I said "yes" to the opportunity.

In hindsight, the deep significance and groundbreaking nature of my placement was all around me. Giant signs that I looked past. The offer of the "off schedule" session with other Black professionals was a career first. I interpreted that as a cutting-edge DEI practice indicating to me that members of the committee recognized that my lived experience as a resident in the city and state might be starkly different from theirs. The after-dinner conversation where a future white male colleague asked how I anticipated handling being the only Black female at a leadership table that includes five white men was a bit disarming. Because my diversity definition is broader than the color of one's skin, the presence of three women and a Latinx man on the leadership team also represented visible diverse perspectives. I diplomatically, firmly shared that this was not my first experience being a first, only, different (FOD)—a term coined by the formidable Shonda Rhimes in her book, *Year of Yes: How to Dance It Out, Stand In the Sun and Be Your Own Person*, so the lack of people of color seemed routine in my experience, and something for which I was prepared. I explained with specificity how I had and would continue to navigate that world. The mere utterance of the question should have given me more clarity about the journey ahead.

In a group interview, I was asked how I would address potential DEI concerns with offending senior-level colleagues. The position for which I had applied was not the chief diversity officer, so this question was vexing. Were these questions asked of other candidates? All candidates? In the moment, I answered the question with grace, directness, and surety. If offered the position, I knew that I would need to clarify expectations, choose which battles to engage and which to leave behind. These questions weren't intended to be mean or cruel; there seemed to be a genuine curiosity. There was some signal that my presence might disrupt or challenge the status quo, behavioral norms, and expectations at the institution. There was sincere interest in how I would handle challenges and the degree to which they'd have to endure discomfort in the process. There also seemed to be a regard for my feelings of safety, happiness, comfort, and success.

Being a FOD—a first, only, different—wasn't new territory. These monikers had been my faithful companions as I entered spaces and places not designed with me in mind. It was my normal. While I saw, heard, and felt the whispers around me as I interviewed, they did not cause trepidation.

There was, however, a depth of the significance of my hire that I did not see. It would not be fully revealed until months after I joined the team. When I met Kevin, the Black custodian who prepared my office for my arrival, he told me he had shown up for my interview and knew that I was the one. He said he prayed over my office and for my resilience and success because "We need you." At that point, the significance of my hire was a faint whisper.